# Comprehensive Conservation Plan
## *Bear Butte National Wildlife Refuge*

**September 2007**

**Prepared by the U.S. Fish and Wildlife Service**

Bear Butte National Wildlife Refuge
29746 Bird Road
Martin, SD 57551

and

U.S. Fish and Wildlife Service, Region 6
Division of Refuge Planning
PO Box 25486 DFC
Lakewood, CO 80225

**Approved by:**

_____     _____
Date

Regional Director, Region 6
U.S. Fish and Wildlife Service
Lakewood, CO

**Submitted by:**

_(signature: Tom Koerner)_      9/24/07

Tom Koerner, Refuge Manager      Date
Bear Butte easement NWR
Martin, SD

**Concurred with:**

Acting _(signature: Dave Linehan)_      9/24/07

Rod Krey      Date
Refuge Program Supervisor (ND, SD)
U.S. Fish and Wildlife Service, Region 6
Lakewood, CO

and

_(signature: Lance R. Kuester)_      09/24/07

Acting    Richard A. Coleman, Ph.D.      Date
Assistant Regional Director
National Wildlife Refuge System
U.S. Fish and Wildlife Service, Region 6
Lakewood, CO

# Contents

## Appendices

# List of Figures and Tables

## Figures

## Tables

# Abbreviations

| | |
|---|---|
| BLM | Bureau of Land Management |
| CCP | comprehensive conservation plan |
| CD | compatibility determination |
| EA | environmental assessment |
| EO | executive order |
| FONSI | finding of no significant impact |
| Improvement Act | National Wildlife Refuge System Improvement Act of 1997 |
| NEPA | National Environmental Policy Act of 1969 |
| NOI | notice of intent |
| refuge | Bear Butte National Wildlife Refuge |
| Refuge System | National Wildlife Refuge System |
| SDGFP | South Dakota Game, Fish, and Parks Department |
| Service or USFWS | U.S. Fish and Wildlife Service |
| state | state of South Dakota |

Bear Butte National Wildlife Refuge (NWR) was established as a limited-interest refuge in the late 1930s with the acquisition of easements from private landowners, the state of South Dakota, and the War Department (now transferred to the Bureau of Land Management at Fort Meade) to maintain an area for "migratory bird, wildlife conservation, and other purposes." The refuge is 374.20 easement acres and has no fee title.

The U.S.. Fish and Wildlife Service entered into a cooperative agreement with the state of South Dakota on July 12, 1967, to administer, operate, and maintain the refuge pursuant to the rights and interests in real property acquired by the United States, and more particularly described in the easement agreement (see appendix F).

This comprehensive conservation plan and environmental assessment (CCP/EA) has been prepared by a planning team consisting of representatives from various U.S. Fish and Wildlife Service programs, including the refuge staff, and in consultation with the South Dakota Game, Fish, and Parks Department (SDGFP). See appendix A for a list of planning team members and contributors.

## PURPOSES OF ESTABLISHMENT

The purposes of the refuge are as follows:

*Executive Order, August 26, 1935,* "as a refuge and breeding ground for migratory birds and other wildlife."

*Migratory Bird Conservation Act* "for use as an inviolate sanctuary, or for any other management purpose, for migratory birds."

## THE PLANNING PROCESS

This final CCP/EA for the refuge was mandated by the National Wildlife Refuge System Improvement Act of 1997.

## ALTERNATIVES

Two alternatives were developed during the planning process. Alternative A—current management (no action) describes the current and future management of the refuge. Under the preferred alternative, the U.S. Fish and Wildlife Service will continue to manage the refuge within the parameters of the cooperative agreement. Existing habitat within the easement and all public programs will continue to be administered

*American Avocet*

and maintained by SDGFP as per the 1967 cooperative agreement.

Alternative B. proposes relinquishing the easement to current landowners. Under this alternative, Bear Butte NWR will be taken out of the National Wildlife Refuge System and the easements will be transferred to the current landowners. Under this alternative, the U.S. Fish and Wildlife Service's requirements will no longer exist. It will divest its interest in the refuge. This was the proposed action in the draft CCP/EA.

However, after further evaluation and consideration of tribal concerns and issues raised by the public, alternative A—current management (no action) is now the preferred alternative, hence the final CCP. According to refuge planning policy (May 25, 2000), the CCP should be revised when significant new information becomes available. This should occur every 15 years or sooner, if necessary. It is important to note that if conditions change, the Service could reconsider actions approved in the CCP. If revisions were considered, full disclosure through extensive public involvement using the National Environmental Policy Act of 1969 (NEPA) and other compliance procedures would be closely followed.

# 1 Introduction

The U.S. Fish and Wildlife Service (Service) has developed this final comprehensive conservation plan (CCP) for Bear Butte National Wildlife Refuge (the refuge). It meets the intent of the National Wildlife Refuge System (Refuge System) Improvement Act of 1997 (Improvement Act).

The plan was developed in compliance with the Improvement Act and part 602 (Refuge System Planning) of the Service manual. The actions described within this plan also meet the requirements of the National Environmental Policy Act of 1969 (NEPA). Compliance with this act is being achieved through the involvement of the public and the inclusion of an integrated environmental assessment (EA).

The refuge was established as a limited-interest refuge in the late 1930s with the acquisition of easements from private landowners, the state of South Dakota (state), and the War Department, now transferred to Bureau of Land Management at Fort Meade, to maintain an area for "migratory bird, wildlife conservation, and other purposes." The refuge is 374.20 easement acres and has no fee title. The easement obtained from the state only applies to lands below the ordinary high-water mark of the lake. A cooperative agreement was entered into with the state on July 12, 1967, to administer, operate, and maintain the refuge pursuant to the rights and interest in real property acquired by the United States, and more particularly described in the easement agreements (see appendix F).

The plan has been prepared by a planning team composed of representatives from various Service programs, including the refuge staff, and in consultation with the South Dakota Game, Fish, and Parks Department (SDGFP).

After reviewing public comments and management needs, the planning team developed a preferred alternative. A draft CCP was developed and released for public review and comment. The draft CCP listed alternative B as the proposed action, which included divestiture of the limited-interest easements. After reviewing public comments, further evaluation, and taking into account tribal concerns, the final CCP adopted alternative A—current management (no action). This alternative will attempt to address all significant issues while determining how best to achieve the intent and purposes of the refuge. The preferred alternative is the Service's recommended course of action for the future management of this refuge and is embodied in this final CCP/EA.

According to refuge planning policy (May 25, 2000), the CCP should be revised when significant new information becomes available. This should occur every 15 years or sooner, if necessary. It is important to note that if conditions change, the Service could reconsider actions approved in the CCP. If revisions were considered, full disclosure through extensive public involvement using NEPA and other compliance procedures would be closely followed.

## PURPOSE AND NEED FOR PLAN

The purpose of this final CCP/EA is to identify the role that the refuge will play in support of the mission of the Refuge System, and to provide long-term guidance to management programs and activities. The plan is needed to:

- provide a clear statement of direction for future management;
- provide landowners, neighbors, visitors, and government officials with an understanding

*Bear Butte*

Tom Koerner /USFWS

of the Service's management actions on and around this refuge;

- ensure that the Service's management actions are consistent with the mandates of the Improvement Act of 1997, and;

- ensure that the management of this refuge is consistent with federal, state, and county plans.

## THE U.S. FISH AND WILDLIFE SERVICE AND THE NATIONAL WILDLIFE REFUGE SYSTEM

### THE U.S. FISH AND WILDLIFE SERVICE

*"The mission of the U.S. Fish and Wildlife Service is working with others to conserve, protect, and enhance fish, wildlife, plants, and their habitats for the continuing benefit of the American people."*

Today, the Service enforces federal wildlife laws, manages migratory bird populations, restores nationally significant fisheries, conserves and restores vital wildlife habitat, protects and recovers endangered species, and helps other governments with conservation efforts. It also administers a federal aid program that distributes hundreds of millions of dollars to states for fish and wildlife restoration, boating access, hunter education, and related projects across America.

### THE NATIONAL WILDLIFE REFUGE SYSTEM

In 1903 President Theodore Roosevelt designated the 5.5-acre Pelican Island in Florida as the nation's first wildlife refuge for the protection of brown pelicans and other native nesting birds. This was the first time the federal government set aside land for the sake of wildlife. This small but significant designation was the beginning of the Refuge System. One hundred years later, this system has become the largest collection of lands in the world specifically managed for wildlife, encompassing over 96 million acres within 544 refuges and over 3,000 small areas for waterfowl breeding and nesting. Today, there is at least one refuge in every state in the nation, as well as in Puerto Rico, Guam, and the U.S. Virgin Islands.

In 1997, the Improvement Act established a clear mission for the Refuge System.

*"The mission of the National Wildlife Refuge System is to administer a national network of lands and waters for the conservation, management, and where appropriate, restoration of the fish, wildlife, and plant resources and their habitats within the United States for the benefit of present and future generations of Americans."*

The Improvement Act further states that each refuge shall:

- fulfill the mission of the Refuge System;
- fulfill the individual purposes of each refuge;
- consider the needs of fish and wildlife first;

- develop a CCP for each unit of the Refuge System, and fully involve the public in the preparation of these plans;

- maintain the biological integrity, diversity, and environmental health of the Refuge System;

- recognize that wildlife-dependent recreational activities, including hunting, fishing, wildlife observation and photography, and environmental education and interpretation, are legitimate and priority public uses, and

- retain the authority of refuge managers to determine compatible public uses.

In addition to the overall mission of the Refuge System, the wildlife and habitat vision for each refuge stresses the following principles:

- Fish and wildlife come first.

- Ecosystems, biodiversity, and wilderness are vital concepts in refuge management.

- Refuges must be healthy.

- Growth of refuges must be strategic.

- The Refuge System serves as a model for habitat management with broad participation from others.

Following passage of the Improvement Act, the Service immediately began efforts to carry out the direction of the new legislation, including the preparation of CCPs for all refuges. The development of these plans is now occurring nationally. Consistent with the Improvement Act, all refuge CCPs are being prepared in conjunction with public involvement, and each refuge is required to complete its own plan within the 15-year schedule (by 2012).

### DECISION

The Mountain–Prairie regional director of the Service has selected the alternative that will be implemented as the refuge's CCP. This decision has been made in recognition of the environmental effects of each alternative considered. The decision is disclosed in a finding of no significant impact (FONSI). Implementation of the CCP will begin once the regional director has signed the FONSI (see appendix D).

### PEOPLE AND THE NATIONAL WILDLIFE REFUGE SYSTEM

The nation's fish and wildlife heritage contributes to the quality of American lives. Wildlife and wild places provide special opportunities to recreate, relax, and enjoy the natural world. People and nature are linked through spiritual, recreational, and cultural ties.

## ECOSYSTEM DESCRIPTIONS AND THREATS

### MISSOURI RIVER MAIN STEM

The Service has adopted watersheds as the basic building blocks for implementing ecosystem conservation. The refuge is located in the Missouri River main stem ecosystem. This vast area covers all of North Dakota and South Dakota and small portions of Montana, Nebraska, and Wyoming. The major threats identified for this ecosystem include conversion of prairie to cropland, overgrazing, invasive species, and aggressive prairie-dog control. The Service contributes to the accomplishment of goals for this ecosystem through its Partners for Fish and Wildlife Program.

## NATIONAL AND REGIONAL MANDATES

The administration of the Refuge System is guided by a variety of international treaties, federal laws, and presidential executive orders (EOs). Management options under each refuge's establishing authority and the Improvement Act are contained in the documents and acts (see appendix B).

## THE PLANNING PROCESS

This final CCP/EA complies with the Improvement Act and NEPA and their implementing regulations. The Service issued a final refuge planning policy in

2000 that established requirements and guidance for Refuge System planning, including CCPs, ensuring that planning efforts comply with the provisions of the Improvement Act. The planning policy identified several steps of the CCP and EA process (see figure 1):

- Form a planning team and conduct preplanning.

- Initiate public involvement and scoping.

- Draft vision statement and goals and determine significant issues.

- Develop and analyze alternatives, including proposed action.

- Prepare draft CCP and EA.

- Prepare and adopt final CCP and EA and issue a FONSI (or determine whether an environmental impact statement is needed).

- Implement plan, monitor, and evaluate.

- Review plan (every 5 years) and revise (every 15 years).

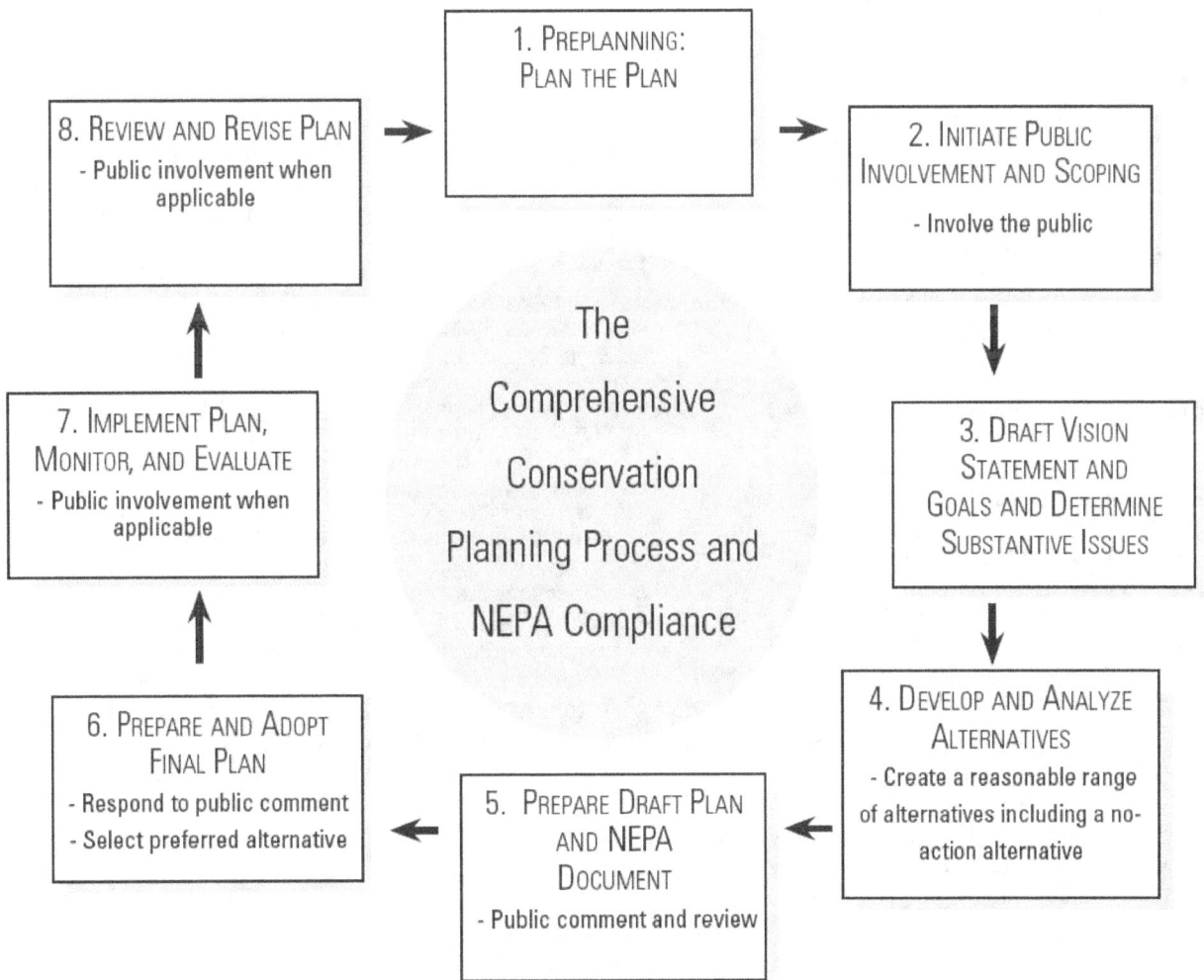

Figure 1. The steps in the CCP planning process

The Service began the preplanning process in September 2004. The refuge is part of the Lacreek National Wildlife Refuge Complex, headquartered near Martin, South Dakota. A planning team comprised of Service personnel from the Lacreek NWR was developed shortly after the initial kickoff meeting (there are currently no Service personnel at Bear Butte NWR). The planning team developed issues and qualities lists.

A notice of intent was published in the "Federal Register" on November 30, 2004. Notification of a public open house was distributed through media press releases.

In October 2004, the region 6 regional director invited the director of the SDGFP to participate in the CCP. The local SDGFP wildlife managers and the Bear Butte State Park manager met with the refuge staff and planning team in early December to discuss the CCP process and the state park operations. They held a public meeting later that October evening in Sturgis, South Dakota. The refuge manager has contacted the Bureau of Land Management and state park personnel throughout the course of the project.

The regional director also sent letters to 24 Native American tribal governments in the northern plains informing them of the upcoming CCP project and inviting them to serve on the core team. Representatives from the Rosebud and Oglala Sioux tribes attended a public open house in Martin, South Dakota, on November 30, 2004, and provided input for the CCP planning team.

The refuge biologist attended a meeting in March 2005 that included all the tribal Game and Fish departments in the Dakotas and Montana. The group had no objections to the state managing fish and wildlife resources on the refuge.

On April 9, 2005, the refuge biologist attended an annual meeting between the SDGFP and several tribes to discuss issues related to Bear Butte State Park and surrounding lands. At that meeting the biologist informed the tribes of the easement refuge the Lacreek NWR Complex has on Bear Butte Lake and the CCP process. Approximately 40 people were in attendance representing three tribes from South Dakota (Standing Rock, Rosebud, and Pine Ridge) and the Northern Cheyenne tribe of Montana. Also in attendance were a state legislator and four SDGFP representatives.

The biologist explained how the easement was acquired, what the easement allows the Service to do, and the cooperative agreement with the state. The biologist then presented the alternatives and asked for verbal and written comments, as part of the public outreach process for the CCP.

*Sandhill Crane*

© 2005 Laura Crawford Williams

During the discussion, the biologist was asked how many acres around the lake itself are under the easement and what the divestiture will involve. Two individuals, representing distinct constituencies, indicated that they would like the Service to maintain the easement. They want to protect the area from development and believe the Service's retaining the easement could serve that purpose. The biologist asked them to provide written comments for the record.

Over the course of preplanning and scoping, the planning team collected information about the resources of the refuge and the surrounding areas. This information is summarized in chapter 4.

A draft CCP was developed and released for public review and comment. An open house was held in Sturgis on February 28, 2007, at the Community Center. Ten individuals attended representing state, county, tribal, local conservation organizations, and landowners interests. In addition, nearly 90 comment letters were received as well as phone calls. These comments were all reviewed by the planning team and taken into consideration (see appendix C).

# 2 The Limited-interest Refuge

## ESTABLISHMENT, ACQUISITION, AND MANAGEMENT HISTORY

The easement refuge is almost identical to other easements acquired during the 1930s that established the right to impound water and close the area to hunting. During this period, the United States faced the Great Depression, a massive drought, and declining waterfowl and wildlife populations. To address this problem, the federal government developed limited-interest refuges through easement agreements with private landowners and states. Originally, easements were purchased from private landowners; however, almost the entire refuge boundary under easement is now owned by the state. A small area within the refuge boundary is not owned by the state, but is also not under an easement.

It is important to note that a small area within the approved refuge boundary has never had an easement acquired. These easements were not needed to complete the dam, impound water, or complete the recreational developments, so they were not pursued.

## CURRENT STATUS OF THE LIMITED-INTEREST REFUGE

The Bear Butte limited-interest refuge is currently owned and operated by the state as part of the Bear Butte State Park, which is part of the state park system. Nearly all of the Bear Butte limited-interest refuge is currently owned in fee title and managed by the SDGFP as part of Bear Butte State Park or the Bureau of Land Management as part of Bear Butte Recreation Area. The butte itself is sacred to many American Indian tribes who come here to hold religious ceremonies. Mato Paha, or Bear Mountain, is the Lakota name for the site.

The butte is located on the east side of Highway 79. It is within the boundaries of Bear Butte State Park but is not on the refuge. Visitors can learn the geological story of this volcano-like structure, its role as a pioneer landmark, and its continuing role as a sacred mountain and founding place of religion for several plains tribes when visiting the Bear Butte Education Center.

The butte has a 1.75-mile limestone-surface trail that ascends from the foot of Bear Butte to its 4,426-foot summit. Designated a National Recreational Trail, it is maintained by state park personnel. Visitors can view four states from the butte's summit, which is also the north end of the Centennial Trail that meanders through the east-central Black Hills and extends 111 miles south to Wind Cave National Park.

*Red-winged Blackbird*

© 2005 Laura Crawford Williams

Bear Butte Lake, which lies in the limited-interest refuge, is where the cooperative agreement is implemented. The state manages a campground and picnic area at the lake and provides opportunities for fishing, hiking, and horseback riding as part of the state park.

Bear Butte State Park is home to a small herd of bison.

### REFUGE PURPOSE
The purposes of the refuge are as follows:

- Executive Order, August 26, 1935, "*as a refuge and breeding ground for migratory birds and other wild animals.*"
- Migratory Bird Conservation Act "*for use as an inviolate sanctuary, or for any other management purpose, for migratory birds.*"

In addition to the legal drivers listed above, the refuge was established under the easement agreement in the late 1930s. As part of the purpose of the refuge the easement reads, "*The exclusive and perpetual right and easement to flood with water, and to maintain and operate a natural or artificial lake thereon or in connection with other land included in what is known as the Bear Butte Lake Project, and to raise the water level thereof by means of dams, dikes, fill, ditches, spillways, and other structures, for water conservation, drought relief, and for migratory bird and wildlife conservation purposes and to operate upon said lands and waters and maintain a wildlife conservation demonstration unit and a closed refuge and reservation for migratory birds and other wildlife.*" It was stipulated that if the purposes for which the easement was granted were abandoned, the land will revert to the grantors or their successors.

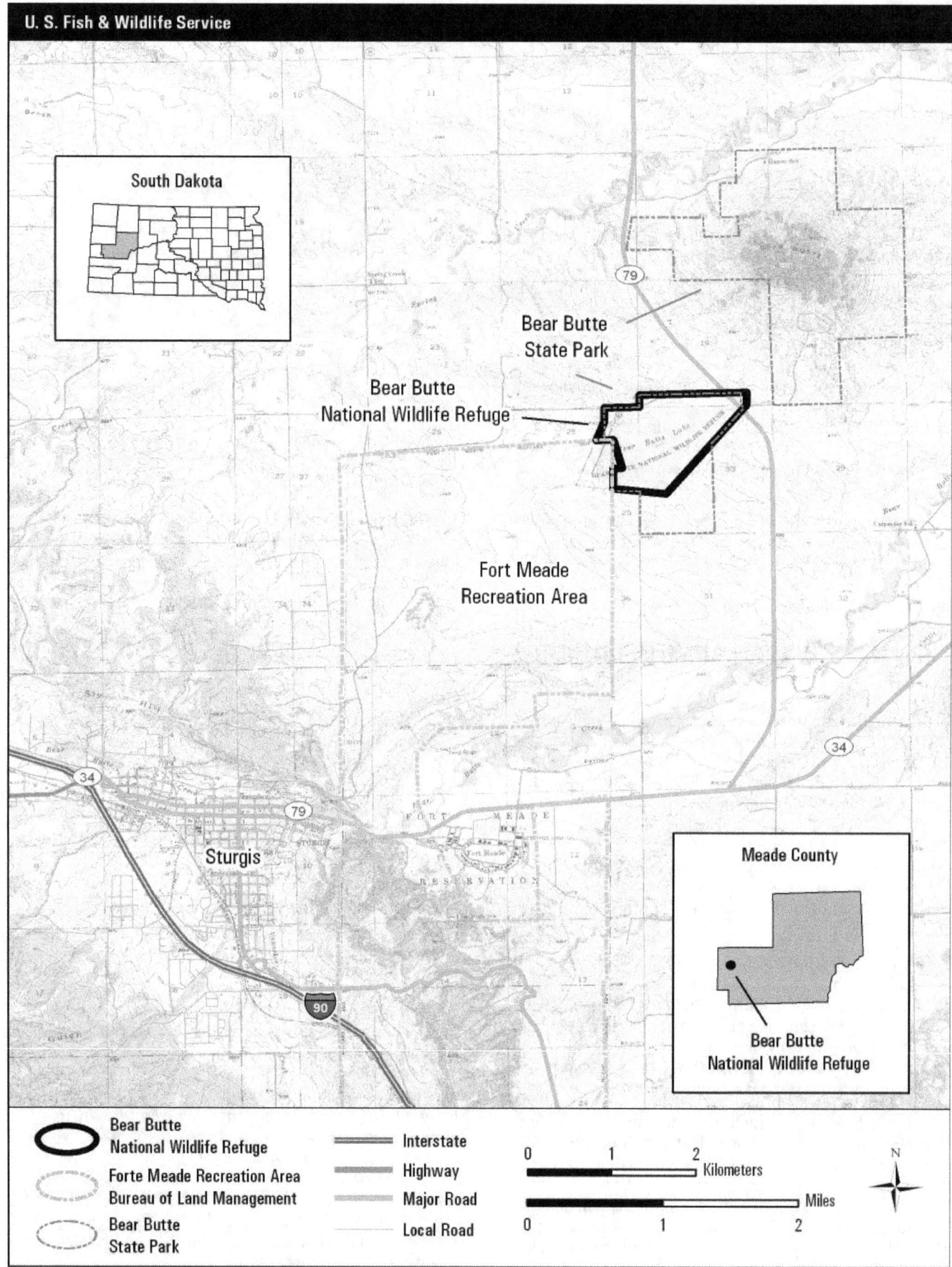

Figure 2. Location map for Bear Butte NWR, South Dakota

## COMPATIBILITY POLICY

Lands within the Refuge System are different from federal, multiple-use public lands, such as National Forest System lands, in that they are closed to all public uses unless specifically and legally opened. The Improvement Act clearly establishes that wildlife conservation is the singular Refuge System mission. To ensure the primacy of the Refuge System's wildlife conservation mission, a compatibility policy was developed and put into effect on November 17, 2000 (http://policy.fws.gov/library/00fr62457.pdf). The compatibility policy states that the Service will not initiate or permit a new use of a refuge or expand, renew, or extend an existing use of a refuge, unless the Service has determined that the use is a compatible use, and that use is not inconsistent with public safety.

A refuge use is defined as any activity on a refuge, except administrative or law enforcement activity, carried out by or under the direction of an authorized Service employee. Recreational uses, including all actions associated with a recreational use, refuge management, economic activities, or other use by the public, are considered to be refuge uses. Facilities and activities associated with recreational public uses, or where there is an economic benefit associated with a use, require compatibility determinations (CDs). Refuge management activities, such as invasive species control, prescribed fire, and scientific monitoring, as well as the facilities for managing a refuge, do not require CDs.

A compatible use is a proposed or existing wildlife-dependent recreational use, or any other use of a refuge that, based on sound professional judgment, will not materially interfere with, or detract from, the fulfillment of the Refuge System mission or the purposes of the refuge. Sound professional judgment is further defined as a decision that is consistent with principles of fish and wildlife management and administration, available science and resources, and adherence to law.

CDs are written determinations signed and dated by the refuge manager and the refuge supervisor stating that a proposed or existing use of a refuge is, or is not, a compatible use. CDs are typically completed as part of the CCP or step-down management plan process. Draft CDs are open to public input and comment. Once a final CD is made by the refuge manager, it is not subject to administrative appeal.

A CD is not required when the Service does not have jurisdiction over the use. Jurisdiction is not to be viewed as what type of law enforcement jurisdiction the Service has over the refuge (i.e., proprietary or concurrent); rather, it asks the question of whether the Service has the legal authority to prohibit a use.

Property rights that are not vested in the federal government must be recognized and allowed whether or not the use might be compatible. In these cases CDs should not be done because the finding is moot, and because the determination may be misinterpreted to mean an activity that otherwise will not be compatible is found to be compatible under certain "circumstances."

Compatibility determinations are usually prepared and provided for public review and comment in the draft CCP/EA. However, since the proposed action in the draft CCP/EA recommended divestiture, CDs were not prepared. A public notice was prepared and disseminated to the public requesting that they review and provide comments on the draft CDs. The final CDs are found in appendix G. They reflect public comments and recognize that the SDGFP is managing the area based on the 1967 cooperative agreement.

## VISION AND GOALS

The planning team developed a vision and a set of goals for the refuge. The vision describes what the refuge will be, or what the Service hopes to do, and is based on the Refuge System mission and purposes of Bear Butte NWR.

Tom Koerner/USFWS

*Bridge*

## VISION

The refuge is located in the foothills of the Black Hills, adjacent to Bear Butte, a sacred site for several Northern Plains tribes. Management will work with partners to protect the cultural significance of the area and to maintain its natural resource values. Opportunities to enjoy wildlife-dependent recreation shall continue to be available to all visitors.

## GOALS

The goals are descriptive, broad statements of desired future condition of the refuge. Four goals were identified for the refuge:

1. *Wildlife and Habitat Management:* Work with partners to maintain habitat for migratory birds and other wildlife.

2. *Public Use:* Work with partners to provide opportunities for quality wildlife-dependent recreation and to promote awareness of the area's resources.

3. *Cultural Resources:* Recognize the cultural significance and sacredness of the Bear Butte area to plains tribes.

4. *Partnerships:* Support existing partnerships that protect the cultural significance of the area, maintain natural resource values, and manage visitor use.

## REFUGE AND RESOURCE DESCRIPTION

### SPECIAL VALUES

During the vision and goals workshop, the planning team identified the outstanding qualities of the refuge. Qualities are the characteristics and features that are evident when a person visits the refuge.

The refuge lies in a wide valley within the Black Hills region of South Dakota. Its proximity to Bear Butte itself and the surrounding area makes it an appealing place to view the butte from a distance.

Some of the refuge's structures were constructed during the Depression under programs designed by President Franklin D. Roosevelt to rebuild the country's resources. Remnants of that era can be found in the campground, including a former bathhouse, a picnic shelter, stone walls, and the dam structure.

Although no longer running, an artesian well fed Bear Butte Lake in the past and was a unique and special value on the refuge.

### ISSUES

Prior to writing the draft CCP, Service staff and other planning team members met to identify any significant issues that should be addressed in the plan. A public open house, news releases in the local and regional press, an announcement in the "Federal Register," and numerous mailings were conducted to solicit public input on important issues to be addressed. Following are the most significant issues identified during public scoping.

#### Habitat and Wildlife

The Service acquired a limited-interest easement to flood with water and to maintain and operate a natural or artificial lake for migratory birds and conservation purposes. One of the easements also secured the right to develop public use facilities and allow public use at the site. From the beginning, Bear Butte NWR was developed more as a recreation area with many non-wildlife-dependent public use facilities such as a beach, swimming pond, boat ramps, and campground and picnic areas. A more appropriate establishing authority would have been as a recreation area rather than a limited-interest national wildlife refuge.

*Bear Butte NWR*

Tom Koerner / USFWS

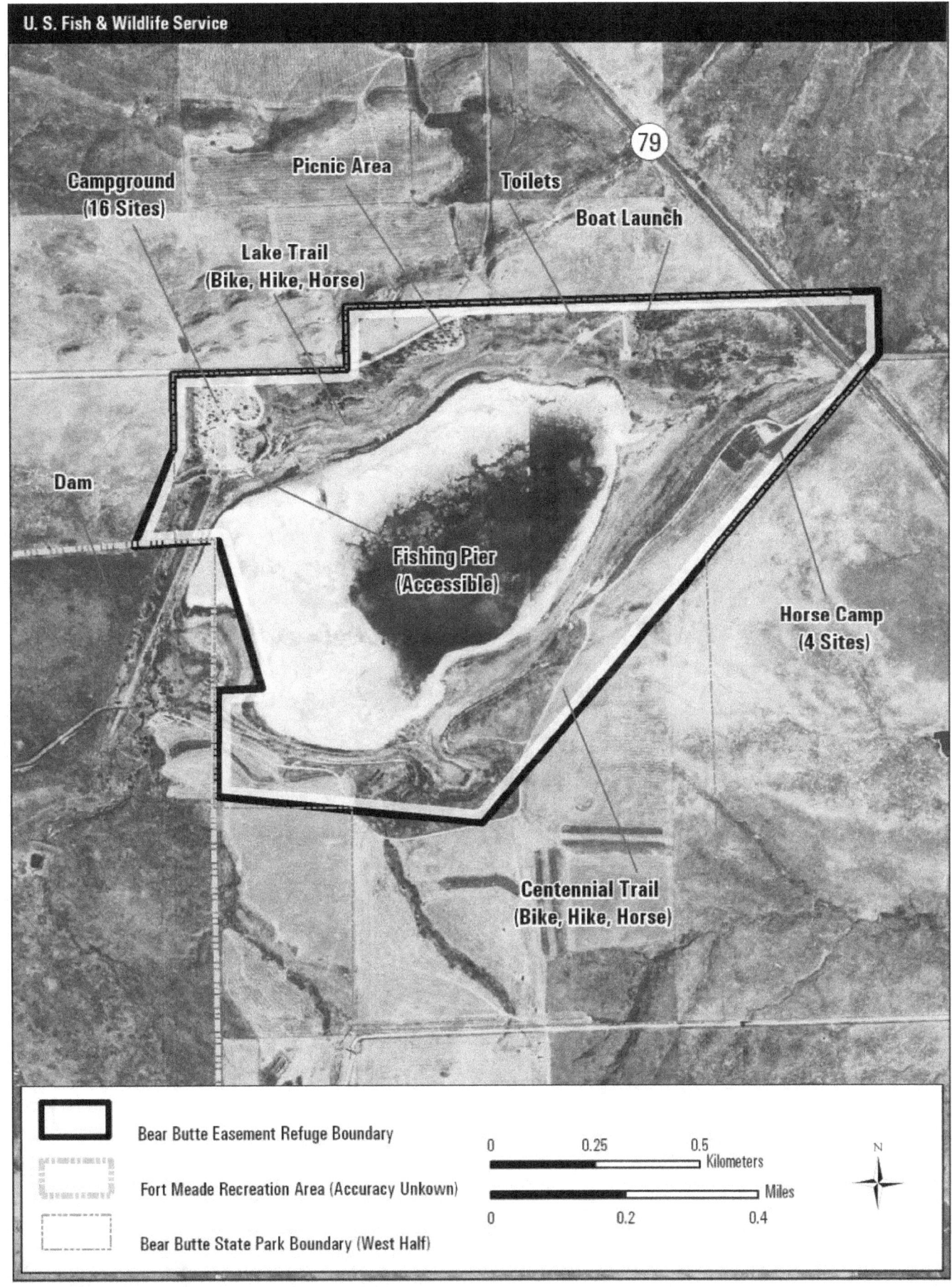

Figure 3. Base map of Bear Butte NWR, South Dakota

During the Depression, however, the Works Progress Administration and the Civilian Conservation Corps were looking for sites to develop water, and this area was one of the few suitable sites west of the Missouri River identified.

### Public Use

The Improvement Act recognized that wildlife-dependent recreational uses—hunting, fishing, wildlife observation and photography, and environmental education and interpretation—when determined to be compatible are legitimate and appropriate public uses of a refuge.

From the beginning, one of the primary purposes intended for the Bear Butte area was recreation. As mentioned earlier, a number of facilities were constructed at about the same time as the dam, to encourage and support camping, swimming, boating, and picnicking.

The Service also has the right to close the area to hunting, and current state park regulations allow hunting on the refuge.

### Water Management

The Bear Butte Lake Project created an artificial lake, which raised water levels by means of an earthen dam and spillway. Originally the lake was filled by an artesian well; however, it stopped flowing and was plugged by the state in May 1987. The water levels are now completely dependent on annual rainfall. The watershed for Bear Butte Lake is relatively small compared to its size. Without supplemental flows of the artesian well, the water levels of the lake have remained low and depend almost entirely on runoff from snow and rain in the local watershed.

### Cultural Resources

The refuge staff recognizes the importance of the cultural resources at the refuge to the Native American community. Refuge staff will continue to work with the state of South Dakota, the BLM, and Native American tribes to preserve these resources for all to enjoy.

### Administration

Limited management activities by the Service have occurred at the refuge since its establishment. As a limited-interest refuge, the Service entered into a cooperative agreement with the state, recognizing that significant cultural and recreational values exist. The Service will continue to work with the state to administer the refuge and maintain the wildlife values that have existed since the refuges establishment.

# 3 Alternatives

## INTRODUCTION

Alternatives are different approaches to management of the refuge. They are designed to resolve issues, achieve the refuge purpose, vision, and goals as identified in the CCP, and fulfill the mission of the Refuge System. They must also comply with current laws, regulations, and policies. NEPA requires an equal and full analysis of all alternatives considered for implementation.

In fall 2004 the Service held a meeting with the public to identify the issues and concerns that were associated with the management of the refuge. The public involvement process is summarized in greater detail in chapter 2. Based on public input, as well as guidelines from NEPA, the Improvement Act, and Service planning policy, the planning team selected the substantive issues that will be addressed in the alternatives. Substantive issues identified for the refuge are:

- habitat and wildlife management
- public use
- water management
- management activities
- cultural resources

A draft CCP/EA was developed and released for public review and comment. An open house was held in Sturgis, South Dakota, on February 28, 2007, at the Community Center. Ten individuals attended representing state, county, tribal, local conservation organizations, and landowners interests. In addition, nearly 90 comment letters were received as well as phone calls. These comments were all reviewed by the planning team and taken into consideration (see appendix C).

The planning team discussed alternatives for management that addressed the substantive refuge issues and met the goals of the Refuge System. Each alternative described in the following sections addresses the substantive issues somewhat differently. Based on further evaluation, consideration of tribal concerns, issues raised by the public, and comments from the initial scoping and the draft public review, alternative A—current management (no action) is the preferred alternative.

According to refuge planning policy (May 25, 2000), the CCP should be revised when significant new information becomes available. This should occur every 15 years or sooner, if necessary. It is important to note that if conditions change, the Service could reconsider actions approved in the CCP. If revisions were considered, full disclosure through extensive public involvement using NEPA and other compliance procedures would be closely followed. The draft CCP/ EA identified alternative B as the proposed action.

This chapter describes two management alternatives for the refuge: the preferred alternative A—current management (no action), and alternative B—relinquish easement to current landowners.

## ALTERNATIVES CONSIDERED BUT ELIMINATED FROM DETAILED STUDY

One alternative the planning team considered would increase the Service's management activities at the refuge. This alternative was rejected because current management of the refuge is provided by the SDGFP, and the area is currently managed as a state park. Increased management by Service personnel would conflict with the state's ability to administer, operate, and maintain the area as they have been doing under the cooperative agreement since 1967.

This alternative was also eliminated from further study because Service personnel determined that it is not feasible to maintain the refuge's habitat alongside the recreational uses (e.g., camping and picnicking) that occur at the park.

The other alternative considered but eliminated from further study was to transfer the easement to another entity. Under the provisions of the easement agreements, however, the Service cannot turn over the easement to any party except the current landowners.

## DESCRIPTION OF ALTERNATIVES

The theme and general management direction for each alternative are described below.

### PREFERRED ALTERNATIVE A—CURRENT MANAGEMENT (NO ACTION)

Under the no-action alternative, the Service would continue to manage the refuge within the parameters of the cooperative agreement with the SDGFP. Existing habitat within the easement and all public programs would continue to be administered and maintained by the state.

Current habitat and wildlife practices would be carried out by park personnel and levels of public use would remain the same. The park facilities and activities—hiking, picnicking, designated camping, fishing, and a horse camp—that are provided on the southeast side of Bear Butte Lake would continue to be offered.

Refuge staff would support partnerships between the state and the tribes for the ongoing protection of cultural resources. The Service would continue passive management and maintenance of facilities (no refuge staff is currently assigned to the station).

### ALTERNATIVE B—RELINQUISH EASEMENT TO CURRENT LANDOWNERS

Alternative B would take the refuge out of the Refuge System and relinquish the easement to the current landowners. Under this alternative, the habitat, public use, cultural resources, and operations would be managed by the landowners. The Service's easement requirements would no longer exist.

The Service would divest its interest in the refuge. This would be carried out within the life of the plan. Once the CCP is approved, the managing station would work with the Service's Division of Realty and the Land Protection Planning Branch within the Division of Planning to prepare a combined program proposal to divest this refuge. The proposal would be submitted to the Migratory Bird Conservation Commission for concurrence and then submitted for congressional approval.

## COMPARISON OF ALTERNATIVES

The two alternatives evaluated in this planning process are: (1) alternative A—current management (no action), and (2) alternative B—relinquish easement to current landowners. A comparison of the alternatives is shown in table 1.

*Bear Butte State Park*

Tom Koerner /USFWS

**Table 1. Comparison of the alternatives**

| Issue | Preferred Alternative A (No Action) | Alternative B (Relinquish Easement to Current Landowners*) |
|---|---|---|
| Habitat and Wildlife | Passive management; maintain existing habitat with easement | The landowners have sole responsibility to manage habitat and wildlife |
| Public Use | Continue to allow the state, the Bureau of Land Management, and private landowner to manage all public-use programs | Same as A |
| Cultural Resources | Support partnerships between the state and the tribes for the ongoing protection of cultural resources | The landowners have sole responsibility to protect cultural resources |
| Operations and Maintenance | Passive management and no maintenance | The landowners are responsible for operations and maintenance |
| Partnerships | Continue to work with state, tribal, and federal partners | Continue to work with state, tribal, and federal partners |
| Easement Rights | Maintain the right to impound water | All easement rights, including the right to impound water, would be voluntarily relinquished to the state |

* i.e. the SDGFP and other current landowners

# 4  Affected Environment

## GENERAL OVERVIEW OF REFUGE

The refuge is six miles northeast of Sturgis, South Dakota, and is part of the Lacreek National Wildlife Refuge Complex headquartered in Martin, South Dakota. The refuge is within the boundary of Bear Butte State Park and is managed by the SDGFP. Sacred to the plains Indian tribes, the butte itself is the place where the god Maheo imparted to Sweet Medicine (a mythical hero) the knowledge from which the Cheyenne derive their religious, political, social, and economic customs. The butte site is a national natural and historic landmark. It is within the boundaries of Bear Butte State Park but is not on the refuge.

## PHYSICAL ENVIRONMENT

### AIR QUALITY

The National Ambient Air Quality Standards include maximum allowable pollution levels for particulate matter (a measure of microscopic liquid or solid particles that is respirable in the lungs), ozone, sulfur dioxide, nitrogen dioxide, lead, and carbon dioxide.

Air quality in the area of the refuge is considered good, with no nearby manufacturing sites or major air pollution sources. Carbon from automobiles and diesel engines, prescribed fire activities on the refuge, and dust associated with wind-blown sand and dirt from the roadways and fields contribute to particulate matter.

### CLIMATE

January and February are the coldest months of winter. Late winter and early spring is western South Dakota's snow season. March is typically the snowiest month of the year.

Late spring is western South Dakota's rainy season, when the area receives over a third of its annual moisture. Precipitation in May comes mostly in showers. By June, thunderstorms are a common occurrence. June marks the peak of severe weather season.

Mid-summer around the Black Hills is warm and dry with plenty of sunshine. Sporadic afternoon and evening thunderstorms occur nearly every day in the summertime over the Black Hills. They usually produce only brief showers. Rainfall decreases as summer draws to a close.

Sunny, mild days and cool nights are typical during the months of September and October. The average first freeze occurs sometime between late August and

*Mink*

September in the Black Hills. Winter weather starts sometime between November and December in the Black Hills. Snowfall averages about 5 inches each month, but most snow is light, as a typical month has only 2 days when more than 1 inch of snow falls.

### PHYSIOGRAPHIC, GEOGRAPHY, AND SOILS

Bear Butte is a laccolith located in the Black Hills, an area of uplifted Precambrian on the Wyoming–South Dakota state line. Bear Butte is made of magma that never reached the surface to generate an eruption. The magma intruded to a shallow level and then stopped, cooled, crystallized, and solidified. Erosion then stripped the overlying layers of rock away. Bear Butte is at the east end of a linear belt of volcanic centers that continues westward about 60 miles to Devils Tower. The rock is called a trachyte based on its mineral composition, which includes alkali feldspar, with small amounts of biotite, hornblende, and pyroxene. Bear Butte rises 1,253 feet above the surrounding plain.

### WATER RESOURCES

The Bear Butte Lake Project created the limited-interest refuge around Bear Butte Lake. It was a natural lake enhanced through the construction of a dam to capture runoff. An easement was established for the use of all water from an artesian well, which has since stopped flowing, and was abandoned by the state in May 1987. The SDGFP holds Water License #844-1 for 520 cubic feet-per-second from dry draws to stabilize Bear Butte Lake levels for recreational purposes (priority date April 12, 1968).

## BIOLOGICAL RESOURCES

This section describes the existing and potential plant and animal communities in the refuge.

## HABITATS

The refuge's habitats comprise mixed-grass prairie in the uplands with a very rapid transition to a lacustrine, or lake habitat, in the permanently impounded area within the high-water mark behind the dam. The plant community of the mixed-grass prairie is greatly influenced by precipitation and the great annual variability that occurs. The tall-grass prairies to the east receive greater annual precipitation than the short-grass prairies to the west. The plant community of the mixed-grass prairie reflects this difference, with species from both the tall- and short-grass prairies found here. Grasses dominate the uplands, including the native, cool-season species of western wheatgrass (*Pascopyrum smithii*), green needlegrass (*Stipa viridula*), and needle and thread grass (*Stipa comata)*. Exotic cool-season grasses, including smooth bromegrass (*Bromus inermis*), Kentucky bluegrass (*Poa pratensis*), and crested wheatgrass (*Agropyron cristatum*), have invaded the site and make up a significant portion of the plant community.

The remainder of the plant community comprises smaller percentages of the following: slender wheatgrass (*Agropyron caninum*), bluebunch wheatgrass (*Agropyron spicatum*), barnyard grass (*Echinochloa crusgalli*), little bluestem (*Schizachyrium scoparium*), foxtail barley (*Hordeum jubatum*), June grass (*Koeleria pyramidata*), marsh muhly (*Muhlenbergia racemosa*), rough leaf ricegrass (*Oryzopsis asperifolia*), Indian ricegrass (*Oryzopsis hymenoides*), western wheatgrass (*Pascopyrum smithii)*, Timothy (*Phleum pratense*), Canada bluegrass (*Poa compressa*), Canby's bluegrass (*Poa canbyi*), inland bluegrass (*Poa interior*), squirreltail (*Sitanion hystrix*), needle and thread grass (*Stipa comata*), and porcupine grass (*Stipa spartea*).

The lake portion is primarily a deep-water habitat, supporting little to no emergent wetland vegetation. If the ongoing drought continues indefinitely, emergent vegetation such as cattail and hardstem bulrush will likely become established and increase in dominance over time along the lake margins until a large runoff event fills the lake and returns it to deep-water habitat once again.

## AQUATIC HABITAT

The refuge provides aquatic habitat for a range of plants and animals. Western painted turtles, blotched tiger salamander, and the upland chorus frog are found on the refuge. A variety of snakes including the western plains and wandering garter snake are found near water. The eastern yellow-bellied racer, bull snake, and prairie rattlesnake are abundant.

## BIRDS

Bird populations on the refuge are dependent on the use and availability of natural resources, including water levels on the lake. Documentation of bird occurrence and use is not well developed for this refuge. Water birds seen on the refuge include American white pelicans, western grebes, double-crested cormorants, Canada and snow geese, mallards, and blue-winged and green-winged teals. Birds of prey seen on the refuge include Swainson's and red-tailed hawks and American kestrel. Shorebirds include killdeer, lesser yellowlegs, and upland sandpipers. Sharp-tailed grouse, American coot, burrowing owls, and black-billed magpie are also seen on the refuge. Bird use will likely follow a predictable pattern. As the lake remains dry, very shallow water will be found for short periods after rainfall and snow melt events. Shorebird, wading bird, and dabbling duck use will increase. If emergent vegetation becomes well established as a result of the low water conditions, species use will increase for marsh wrens, red-winged blackbirds, and other species that prefer this for nesting and feeding. When water returns after heavy runoff events, submerged aquatic vegetation will return, along with use by diving ducks, American white pelicans, and other species preferring

*Canada geese taking flight*

Tom Koerner/USFWS

this more open water and the habitat it provides. A complete list of birds that occur on the refuge is in appendix E.

### FISH

Bear Butte Lake has a surface area of 180 acres and a maximum depth of 13 feet. The lake is owned and managed by the SDGFP. Currently there are four primary game and forage and four secondary species of fish that occur in the lake. An extended drought completely dried up the lake in the late winter of 2006–07. As a result, the game fisheries was lost. When the lake fills again from a significant runoff event and weather patterns appear to be able to provide average rainfall to maintain water levels, the state may consider restocking the lake with game fish species. When there was sufficient water in the lake the primary game fish are large mouth bass, yellow perch, black crappie, and northern pike. Secondary species are green sunfish, fathead minnow rock bass, and black bullhead.

### MAMMALS

Mammals that occur on the refuge include the common raccoon, black-tailed prairie dog, northern pocket gopher, deer mouse, eastern cottontail and whitetail deer, and bison.

### THREATENED AND ENDANGERED SPECIES

There have been no official confirmed sightings of whooping cranes, although they do occur in Meade County. When the lake is full and boating and camping are at a peak, the water depth is not hospitable for cranes; they are much more likely to use the lake when the water level is low and boating is difficult to impossible, and public use is low as a result. The bald eagle was removed from the federal list of threatened and endangered wildlife and plants in August 2007. The bald eagles is listed as a state threatened species.

## CULTURAL RESOURCES

The region is sacred to Native Americans of the plains who consider the Black Hills to be the *axis mundi*, the center of the world.

Bear Butte's geological feature was an important landmark and religious site for plains Indian tribes dating back 10,000 years, well before Europeans reached South Dakota, and it continues to be today. The Lakota also call Bear Butte Mato Paha, or Bear Mountain. To the Cheyenne, it is Noahvose. The mountain is sacred to many indigenous peoples, who make pilgrimages to pray and leave prayer ties on the branches of trees along the trail that leads to the top of the butte.

Notable tribal leaders including Red Cloud, Crazy Horse, and Sitting Bull have all visited Bear Butte. These visits culminated with an 1857 gathering of many Native American nations to discuss the advancement of white settlers into the Black Hills.

U.S. Army cavalry commander George A. Custer, who led an expedition of over a thousand men into the region, camped near the mountain. Custer verified the rumors of gold in the Black Hills. Bear Butte then served as a landmark that helped guide the rush of invading prospectors and settlers into the region.

## SPECIAL MANAGEMENT AREAS

### WILDERNESS

To be designated a wilderness area, lands must meet certain criteria as outlined in the Wilderness Act of 1964:

- Generally appear to have been affected primarily by the forces of nature, with the imprint of human work substantially unnoticeable;

- Have outstanding opportunities for solitude, or a primitive and unconfined type of recreation;

- Have at least 5,000 acres of land, or be of sufficient size as to make practicable its preservation and use in an unimpaired condition, and;

- May also contain ecological, geological, or other features of scientific, educational, scenic, or historical value.

Bear Butte National Wildlife Refuge does not meet the criteria for a wilderness area.

Bear Butte itself was placed on the National Register of Historic Places in 1973 and became a national natural landmark in 1965. The National Natural Landmark program recognizes and encourages the conservation of outstanding examples of our country's natural history. It is the only natural areas program of national scope that identifies and recognizes the best examples of biological and geological features in both public and private ownership.

The trail leading to the summit is designated a national recreation trail. As part of the George S. Mickelson Trail, which spans 114 miles across four counties, this "crown jewel" of the state park system provides a unique educational and recreational experience for visitors of all ages. Winding through the heart of the Black Hills with numerous bridges and tunnels, this rail-trail brings to life the area's rich history with stories of Native Americans, miners, railroad workers, and many others.

Due to the configuration of the refuge within the state park, it does not have these designations as a national register property, national natural landmark, or a national recreation trail.

## VISITOR SERVICES

Because the refuge is located within Bear Butte State Park, a number of park facilities exist. The park offers a hiking trail around Bear Butte Lake; 16 nonelectric campsites; fishing for bullheads, crappies, and northern pike; and the use of boats with 25-horsepower or smaller motors. There is a wheelchair-accessible fishing dock. A horse camp is provided on the southeast side of the lake. Two miles of natural trail exists around Bear Butte Lake; however, horseback riding is only allowed west of Highway 79. The park's hiking trail connects to Centennial Trail, which leads horseback riders through the Black Hills. The horse camp with primitive sites, water, and corral is available on a first-come, first-served basis only. Hunting, especially deer and waterfowl, is very popular in the area. The state does not allow hunting in some sections of the park; however, hunting on open areas of the state park occur on a very infrequent basis. Uncased firearms and bows are prohibited year-round in the designated campground and within the park east of Highway 79.

## SOCIOECONOMIC ENVIRONMENT

This section characterizes current socioeconomic conditions in Meade County, South Dakota.

Bear Butte is located in Meade County, South Dakota. According to the 2000 census, the county has a population of 24,253–8,805 households and 6,700 families. The average household size is 2.66 and the average family size is 3.05. The racial makeup of the county is 92.65% white, 2.10% Hispanic or Latino, 2.04% Native American, 1.48% black or African American, 0.63% Asian, 0.07% Pacific Islander, 0.61% from other races, and 2.52% from two or more races. According to the 2000 census, educational, health and social services are the largest industries, followed by retail-trade arts, entertainment, recreation, accommodation, and food services. The median family income is $40,537 per year.

Hard-surfaced state and federal highways bisect the county in both north-south and east-west directions.

Sturgis is the nearest city to the state park and the refuge. As of the 2000 census, the city had a total population of 6,442. The median income for a household in the city is $30,253 and the median income for a family is $38,698. The racial make up is similar to the rest of the county.

Every August the city hosts one of the largest annual motorcycle events in the world. The campground at Bear Butte State Park is used by motorcycle enthusiast during the motorcycle rally. The number of campground and state park users increase during this period.

*Picnic Shelter*

Tom Koerner /USFWS

# 5  Environmental Consequences

This section analyzes and discusses the potential environmental effects or consequences that can be expected by the implementation of each management alternative described in chapter 3. Table 2 gives a comparison of the environmental consequences of each alternative.

## EFFECTS COMMON TO ALL ALTERNATIVES

### ENVIRONMENTAL JUSTICE
Environmental justice refers to the principle that all citizens and communities are entitled to:

- equal protection from environmental, occupational health, or safety hazards;

- equal access to natural resources, and;

- equal participation in the environmental and natural resource policy formulation process.

On February 11, 1994, President Clinton issued EO 12898: Federal Actions to Address Environmental Justice in Minority Populations and Income Populations. The purpose of this order is to focus the attention of federal agencies on human environmental health and to address inequities that may occur in the distribution of: costs and benefits, land-use patterns, hazardous material transport or facility siting, allocation and consumption of resources, access to information, planning, and decision making.

Within the spirit and intent of EO 12898, no minority or low-income populations will be impacted by any Service action under the two alternatives presented in this document.

### SOCIOECONOMIC IMPACTS
Economic impacts are typically measured in terms of number of jobs lost or gained and the associated result on income. Neither alternative will significantly impact the economics of the local area.

## CUMULATIVE IMPACTS

Cumulative impacts are the potential effects of the action or no-action alternatives in combination with past, present, and future actions. NEPA regulations define cumulative effects "as the impact on the environment which results from the incremental impact of the action when added to other past, present, and reasonably foreseeable future actions regardless of what agency (federal or nonfederal) or person undertakes such other actions. Cumulative impacts can result from individually minor, but collectively significant, actions taking place over time." (40 Code of Federal Regulations 1508.7.)

The cumulative effects analysis for this project is based on reasonably foreseeable future actions that, if implemented, will contribute to the effects of the action or no-action alternative. No reasonably foreseeable actions are anticipated.

## EFFECTS OF ALTERNATIVE A

Under the no-action alternative, the Service will continue to manage the refuge within the parameters of the cooperative agreement with the SDGFP. Existing habitat within the easement and all public programs will continue to be administered and maintained by the state.

### HABITATS AND WILDLIFE
Under alternative A, the refuge will maintain the current habitat management program administered through the cooperative agreement with the state. The uplands and wetlands will be managed as part of the state park, and passive management of the existing habitat within the easement will continue giving the refuge staff little ability to promote species diversity.

Because of multiple uses and alterations of the landscape and the size and connectivity of habitat patches, which makes movement of wildlife or genetic information between parcels of land difficult or impossible, the habitat can no longer support species diversity.

### WATER MANAGEMENT
The water cycle on Bear Butte Lake under both alternatives will continue to be dependent on spring runoff and annual rainfall. The ability to hold water levels and wetland conditions through water management would continue to be dependent on annual precipitation. Water cycle conditions would have little to no effect on current bird populations. There will be no change in existing water-quality conditions and sedimentation trends.

### PUBLIC USE
All public programs are administered by the state under alternative A. Conflicting purposes of the state and the Service do not allow the Service to provide opportunities for the six priority public-use activities. The state, for example, provides campgrounds within the refuge boundary. Campgrounds are not a priority use on refuges nor are they wildlife compatible or wildlife dependent, and as such are generally not allowed. In a few situations they are allowed to support priority public uses, but in this case camping does not support these uses.

Current on- and off-refuge opportunities for wildlife viewing, education, and interpretation will be retained. This includes informational kiosks, hiking trails, day-use areas, a fishing platform, and educational programs. These programs will continue to place an emphasis on the state park and its programs. Visitors will not be aware that they are visiting a refuge.

Under alternative A, there will be no change in current management of hunting and fishing opportunities.

### CULTURAL RESOURCES

Under alternative A, there will be no changes to cultural resource management. Current management activities will continue to be carried out solely by the state under the cooperative agreement.

### OPERATIONS AND MAINTENANCE

Under alternative A, there will be no change in current operations and maintenance activities.

### SOCIOECONOMIC IMPACTS

Under alternative A, there will be no change in socioeconomic climate.

## EFFECTS OF ALTERNATIVE B

Under alternative B, the refuge will be taken out of the Refuge System (divested) and transferred to the state. Under this alternative, the habitat, public use, cultural resources, and operations will be managed by the landowners. The Service's easement requirements will no longer exist. The Service will divest its interest in the refuge.

### HABITATS AND WILDLIFE

Since the state currently maintains habitats and wildlife, there will be no change. The cooperative agreement will no longer be in place and easement will be removed.

### WATER MANAGEMENT

Since the state is currently responsible for water issues, there will be no change. The cooperative agreement will no longer be in place and easement will be removed.

### PUBLIC USE

Since the state is currently responsible for issues relating to public use, there will be no change. The cooperative agreement will no longer be in place and easement will be removed.

### CULTURAL RESOURCES

Since the state is currently responsible for issues relating to cultural resources, there will be no change. The cooperative agreement will no longer be in place and easement will be removed.

### OPERATIONS AND MAINTENANCE

Since the state is currently responsible for operations and maintenance, there will be no change. The cooperative agreement will no longer be in place and easement will be removed.

### SOCIOECONOMIC IMPACTS

Since there will be no change to the aforementioned categories, there should not be any change to the socioeconomic impact.

Bear Butte NWR

Tom Koerner/USFWS

**Table 2. Description of consequences by alternative**

| Issue | Preferred Alternative A (no action) | Alternative B |
|---|---|---|
| Habitats and Wildlife | Continued reliance on state to manage habitats and wildlife. | Same as A except cooperative agreement would no longer be in place and easement would be removed. |
| Water Management | Continued dependence on annual rainfall. Continued emphasis on providing recreational activities. No change in existing water-quality conditions and sedimentation trends. | Same as A except cooperative agreement would no longer be in place and easement would be removed. |
| Public Use | Review existing non-wildlife-dependent recreation uses for compliance with the Improvement Act and accompanying regulations and policies through a CD process. | Current public-use activities, including non-wildlife-dependent activities, would continue. Non compliance with Improvement Act would no longer be an issue. |
| Cultural Resources | The state will continue to manage the cultural resources. | Same as A except cooperative agreement would no longer be in place. |
| Operations and Maintenance | Continue current level of operations and maintenance under cooperative agreement. | Current operations and maintenance activities would continue. |
| Socioeconomic Impacts | No change to socioeconomic climate. | No change to socioeconomic climate. |

# 6 Comprehensive Conservation Plan

*Prairie Dog*
Bob Savannah/USFWS

# 6 Comprehensive Conservation Plan

The future direction for Bear Butte NWR was developed for this final CCP based on careful analysis of information; involvement of federal, tribal, state, and local government contacts, conservation organizations, landowners, and other interested parties; and determining the best course of action for Bear Butte NWR and the community, at large. Alternative A—current management (no action) was selected as the preferred alternative, the final CCP.

Under this alternative, the limited-interest easements will continue to be managed through the 1967 cooperative agreement with the state of South Dakota, with periodic reviews between the Service and state.

## MANAGEMENT SUMMARY

Bear Butte NWR is an atypical refuge compared to most refuges in the Refuge System. As stated throughout this document, the area was established primarily as a recreation area with some wildlife benefits. At the time, establishment of a limited-interest easement refuge was the only avenue available to secure assistance from the Civilian Conservation Corps to construct a dam and recreational facilities. It would have been a much better administrative fit to have placed management of the easements with another land management entity with a mission more aligned with recreational use.

Bear Butte Lake

This unique situation has existed throughout the history of Bear Butte NWR. Indeed, a number of attempts have been made to divest the limited-interest easement refuge, and a solution was sought when the state of South Dakota purchased much of the lands in fee title. Historically, divestiture of any refuge is not easily accomplished, nor is it welcomed by a large segment of the public. Even divestiture of a limited-interest easement refuge that is owned in fee title by other state and federal land-management agencies is frequently not supported.

## MANAGEMENT DIRECTION

After a review of all the public comments received and consideration of tribal concerns raised during the public comment period, it was decided to table attempts at divestiture using the CCP/EA process. According to refuge planning policy (May 25, 2000), the CCP should be revised when significant new information becomes available. This should occur every 15 years or sooner, if necessary. It is important to note that if conditions change, the Service could reconsider actions approved in the CCP. If revisions were considered, full disclosure through extensive public involvement using NEPA and other compliance procedures would be closely followed.

Therefore, the Service will continue to manage the refuge within the parameters of the 1967 cooperative agreement with the South Dakota Game, Fish, and Parks Department (SDGFP). Existing recreational uses, public programs, and habitat within the limited-interest easement refuge will continue to be managed by the SDGFP. Current habitat and wildlife practices will continue to be carried out by state park personnel, and levels of public use will remain the same. The state park facilities and activities that are provided on the southeast side of Bear Butte Lake—hiking, picnicking, designated camping, fishing, and a horse camp—will continue to be offered. Refuge staff will support partnerships between the SDGFP and the tribes for the ongoing protection of cultural resources. The Service will continue passive management and maintenance of facilities. No refuge staff will be assigned to the limited-interest easement refuge, as is currently the case.

The Service has limited authority outside the scope of this limited-interest easement refuge and the 1967 cooperative agreement to prevent or shape the future development and activities conducted on private lands adjacent to and near Bear Butte. Development around the butte is highly controversial. Many local residents and tribal members wish to preserve the site's special values. The Service will continue to encourage pursuit of other avenues for protection of the site's cultural integrity.

# Glossary

*Canada Goose*
Bob Savannah/USFWS

**alternative:** (1) a reasonable way to solve an identified problem or satisfy the stated need (40 CFR 1500.2); (2) alternatives are different means of accomplishing refuge purposes and goals and contributing to the Refuge System mission (Draft Service Manual 602 FW 1.5).

**biological integrity:** Biotic composition, structure and function at genetic, organism and community levels comparable with historic conditions, including the natural biological processes that shape the genomes, organisms, and communities.

**CCP:** *See* comprehensive conservation plan.

**compatible use:** A wildlife-dependent recreational use or any other use of a refuge that, in the sound professional judgment of the director of the U.S. Fish and Wildlife Service, will not materially interfere with or detract from the fulfillment of the mission of the Refuge System or the purposes of the refuge (Draft Service Manual 603 FW 3.6). A compatibility determination supports the selection of compatible uses and identified stipulations or limits necessary to ensure compatibility.

**comprehensive conservation plan (CCP):** A document that describes the desired future conditions of the refuge; and provides long-range guidance and management direction for the refuge manager to accomplish the purposes of the refuge, contribute to the mission of the Refuge System, and to meet other relevant mandates (Draft Service Manual 602 FW 1.5).

**cultural resources:** The remains of sites, structures, or objects used by people in the past.

**easement refuge:** *See* limited-interest national wildlife refuge.

**ecosystem:** A dynamic and interrelating complex of plant and animal communities and their associated non-living environment. A biological community, together with its environment, functioning as a unit. For administrative purposes, the Service has designated 53 ecosystems covering the United States and its possessions. These ecosystems generally correspond with watershed boundaries and their sizes and ecological complexity vary.

**endangered species (federal):** A plant or animal species listed under the Endangered Species Act of 1973 (as amended) that is in danger of extinction throughout all, or a significant portion of, its range.

**endangered species (state):** A plant or animal species in danger of becoming extinct or extirpated in a particular state within the near future if factors contributing to its decline continue. Populations of these species are at critically low levels or their habitats have been degraded or depleted to a significant degree.

**environmental assessment (EA):** A concise public document, prepared in compliance with the National Environmental Policy Act, that briefly discusses the purpose and need for an action, alternatives to such action, and provides sufficient evidence and analysis of impacts to determine whether to prepare an environmental impact statement or finding of no significant impact (40 CFR 1508.9).

**fragmentation:** The alteration of a large block of habitat which creates isolated patches of the original habitat that are interspersed with a variety of other habitat types (Koford et al. 1994); the process of reducing the size and connectivity of habitat patches, making movement of individuals or genetic information between parcels difficult or impossible.

**goal:** Descriptive, open-ended, and often broad statement of desired future conditions that conveys a purpose but does not define measurable units (Draft Service Manual 620 FW 1.5).

**habitat:** Suite of existing environmental conditions required by an organism for survival and reproductions. The place where an organism typically lives and grows.

**habitat disturbance:** Significant alteration of habitat structure or composition. Event may be natural (e.g., fire) or human-caused (e.g., timber harvest, disking).

**habitat type (vegetation type, cover type):** A land classification system based on the concept of distinct plant associations.

**impoundment:** A body of water created by collection and confinement within a series of levees or dikes, thus creating separate management units, although not always independent of one another.

**inviolate sanctuary:** A place of refuge or protection where animals and birds may not be hunted.

**invasive plant:** a species that is nonnative to the ecosystem under consideration and whose introduction causes, or is likely to cause, economic or environmental harm or harm to human health.

**issue:** Any unsettled matter that requires a management decision; e.g., a Service initiative, opportunity, resource management problem, a threat to the resources of the unit, conflict in uses, public concern, or the presence of an undesirable resource condition (Draft Service Manual 602 FW 1.5).

**limited-interest national wildlife refuge:** A national wildlife refuge that has more than 85% of its approved boundary covered by a 1930s flowage easement and/or refuge easement, giving the Service limited management capabilities.

**management alternative:** *See* alternative.

**migration:** Regular extensive, seasonal movements of birds between their breeding regions and their "wintering" regions (Koford et al. 1994); to pass periodically from one region or climate to another for feeding or breeding.

**migratory birds:** Birds that follow a seasonal movement from their breeding grounds to their "wintering" grounds. Waterfowl, shorebirds, raptors, and song birds are all migratory birds.

**mission:** Succinct statement of purpose and/or reason for being.

**mixed-grass prairie:** A transition zone between the tall-grass prairie and the short-grass prairie dominated by grasses of medium height that are approximately 2–4 feet tall. Soils are not as rich as the tall-grass prairie and moisture levels are less.

**national wildlife refuge:** "A designated area of land, water, or an interest in land or water within the Refuge System, but does not include coordination areas." Find a complete listing of all units of the Refuge System in the current *Annual Report of Lands Under Control of the U.S. Fish and Wildlife Service.*

**National Wildlife Refuge System:** Various categories of areas administered by the Secretary of the Interior for the conservation of fish and wildlife, including species threatened with extinction, all lands, waters, and interests therein administered by the Secretary as wildlife refuges, areas for the protection and conservation of fish and wildlife that are threatened with extinction, wildlife ranges, game ranges, wildlife management areas, or waterfowl production areas.

**National Wildlife Refuge System Improvement Act of 1997:** Sets the mission and the administrative policy for all refuges in the Refuge System. Clearly defines a unifying mission for the Refuge System; establishes the legitimacy and appropriateness of the six priority public uses (hunting, fishing, wildlife observation and photography, and environmental education and interpretation); establishes a formal process for determining appropriateness and compatibility; establish the responsibilities of the Secretary of the Interior for managing and protecting the Refuge System; and requires a comprehensive conservation plan for each refuge by the year 2012. This Act amended portions of the Refuge Recreation Act and National Wildlife Refuge System Administration Act of 1966.

**native species:** A species that occurred or currently occurs in that ecosystem and is not the result of human introduction into that ecosystem.

**nongovernmental organization (NGO):** Any group that is not composed of federal, state, tribal, county, city, town, local, or other governmental entities.

**objective:** An objective is a concise target statement of what will be achieved, how much will be achieved, when and where it will be achieved, and who is responsible for the work. Objectives are derived from goals and provide the basis for determining management strategies. Objectives should be attainable and time-specific and should be stated quantitatively to the extent possible. If objectives cannot be stated quantitatively, they may be stated qualitatively (Draft Service Manual 602 FW 1.5).

**plant community:** An assemblage of plant species unique in its composition; occurs in particular locations under particular influences; a reflection or integration of the environmental influences on the site, such as soil, temperature, elevation, solar radiation, slope, aspect, and rainfall; denotes a general kind of climax plant community, i.e., ponderosa pine or bunchgrass.

**proposed action:** The alternative proposed by the Service to best achieve the refuge purpose, vision, and goals; contributes to the Refuge System mission, addresses the significant issues; and is consistent with principles of sound fish and wildlife management.

**priority public use:** One of six uses authorized by the Improvement Act of 1997 to have priority if found to be compatible with a refuge's purposes. This includes hunting, fishing, wildlife observation, and photography, environmental education and interpretation.

**public:** Individuals, organizations, and groups; officials of federal, state, and local government agencies; Indian tribes; and foreign nations. It may include anyone outside the core planning team. It includes those who may or may not have indicated an interest in Service issues and those who do or do not realize that Service decisions may affect them.

**public involvement:** A process that offers affected and interested individuals and organizations an opportunity to learn about Service actions and policies and to express their opinions. The Service gives thoughtful consideration to public opinions when shaping decisions for refuge management.

**purpose of the refuge:** The purpose of a refuge is specified in, or derived from, the law, proclamation, executive order, agreement, public land order, donation document, or administrative memorandum establishing, authorization, or expanding a refuge, refuge unit, or refuge subunit. (Draft Service Manual 602 FW 1.5).

**refuge purpose:** *See* purpose of the refuge.

**refuge use:** Any activity on a refuge, except for an administrative or law enforcement activity, carried out by, or under the direction of, an authorized Service employee.

**restoration:** Management emphasis designed to move ecosystems to desired conditions and processes, and/or to healthy upland habitats and aquatic systems.

**riparian area or zone:** An area or habitat that is transitional from a terrestrial to an aquatic ecosystem—includes streams, lakes wet areas, and adjacent plant communities and their associated soils that have free water at or near the surface; an area whose components are directly or indirectly attributed to the influence of water; of or relating to a river; specifically applied to ecology, "riparian" describes the land immediately adjoining and directly influenced by streams. For example, riparian vegetation includes any and all plant life growing on the land adjoining a stream and directly influenced by the stream.

**scoping:** The process of obtaining information from the public for input into the planning process.

**Service:** *See* U.S. Fish and Wildlife Service.

**shorebird:** Any of a suborder (*Charadrii*) of birds (such as a plover or a snipe) that frequents the seashore or mud flat areas.

**strategy:** A specific action, tool, or technique—or combination of actions, tools, and techniques—used to meet unit objectives (Draft Service Manual 602 FW 1.5).

**U.S. Fish and Wildlife Service (Service, USFWS):** The principal federal agency responsible for conserving, protecting, and enhancing fish and wildlife and their habitats for the continuing benefit of the American people. The Service manages the 93-million-acre Refuge System comprised of more than 530 refuges and thousands of waterfowl production areas. It also operates 65 national fish hatcheries and 78 ecological service field stations, the agency enforces federal wildlife laws, manages migratory bird populations, restores national significant fisheries, conserves and restores wildlife habitat such as wetlands, administers the Endangered Species Act, and helps foreign governments with their conservation efforts. It also oversees the federal aid program, which distributes millions of dollars collected from excise taxes on fishing and hunting equipment to state wildlife agencies.

**U.S. Fish and Wildlife Service mission:** The mission of the U.S. Fish and Wildlife Service is working with others to conserve, protect, and enhance fish, wildlife, plants, and their habitats for the continuing benefit of the American people.

**USFWS:** *See* U.S. Fish and Wildlife Service.

**vision statement:** A concise statement of the desired future condition of the planning unit, based primarily on the Refuge System mission, specific refuge purposes, and other relevant mandates (Draft Service Manual 602 FW 1.5).

**warm-season grasses:** Grasses that begin growth later in the season (early June). These grasses require warmer soil temperatures to germinate and actively grow when temperatures are warmer. Examples of warm season grasses are Indiangrass, switchgrass, and big bluestem.

**waterfowl:** A category of birds that includes ducks, geese, and swans.

**watershed:** The region draining into a river, river system, or body of water.

**wildlife-dependent recreational use:** The six priority public uses of the Refuge System as established in the Improvement Act are: hunting, fishing, wildlife observation and photography, and environmental education and interpretation. The Service also considers other wildlife-dependent uses in the preparation of CCPs; however, the six priority public uses always take precedence.

# Appendices

This plan is the result of the efforts by members of the planning team for Bear Butte NWR. The draft CCP and EA were written by refuge staff and the refuge planning team with input from other team members.

## Planning Team

| Name | Title | Agency |
| --- | --- | --- |
| Linda Kelly | Planning team leader | USFWS |
| Tom Koerner | Project leader | USFWS |
| Shilo Comeau | Refuge biologist | USFWS |

## Other Contributers

| Name | Title | Agency |
| --- | --- | --- |
| Michael Spratt | Chief, division of refuge planning | USFWS |
| Mimi Mather | Landscape architect/planner | Shapins and Associates |
| Tom Gibney | Landscape architect/planner | Shapins and Associates |

## NATIONAL WILDLIFE REFUGE MISSION, GOALS, AND GUIDING PRINCIPLES

The mission of the System is *"to administer a national network of lands and waters for the conservation, management, and where appropriate, restoration of the fish, wildlife, and plant resources and their habitats within the United States for the benefit of present and future generations of Americans"* (National Wildlife Refuge System Improvement Act of 1997).

### GOALS OF THE NATIONAL WILDLIFE REFUGE SYSTEM ARE:

A. To fulfill our statutory duty to achieve refuge purpose(s) and further the System mission.

B. Conserve, restore where appropriate, and enhance all species of fish, wildlife, and plants that are endangered or threatened with becoming endangered.

C. Perpetuate migratory bird, inter-jurisdictional fish, and marine mammal populations.

D. Conserve a diversity of fish, wildlife, and plants.

E. Conserve and restore, where appropriate, representative ecosystems of the United States, including the ecological processes characteristic of those ecosystems.

F. To foster understanding and instill appreciation of fish, wildlife, and plants, and their conservation, by providing the public with safe, high-quality, and compatible wildlife-dependent public use. Such use includes hunting, fishing, wildlife observation and photography, and environmental education and interpretation.

There are four guiding principles for management and general public use of the refuge System established by Executive Order 12996 (3/25/96):

- **Public Use.** The Refuge System provides important opportunities for compatible wildlife-dependent recreational activities involving hunting, fishing, wildlife observation and photography, and environmental education and interpretation.

- **Habitat.** Fish and wildlife will not prosper without high quality habitat, and without fish and wildlife, traditional uses of refuge cannot be sustained. The Refuge System will continue to conserve and enhance the quality and diversity of fish and wildlife habitat within refuges.

- **Partnerships.** America's sportsmen and women were the first partners who insisted on protecting valuable wildlife habitat within wildlife refuges.

Conservation partnerships with other federal agencies, state agencies, tribes, organizations, industry, and the general public can make significant contributions to the growth and management of the System.

- **Public Involvement.** The public should be given a full and open opportunity to participate in decisions regarding acquisition and management of our national wildlife refuges.

### LEGAL AND POLICY GUIDANCE

Management actions on national wildlife refuges are circumscribed by many mandates (laws, Executive Orders, etc.), the latest of which is the Volunteer and Community Partnership Enhancement Act of 1998. Regulations that affect refuge management the most are listed below.

**National Historic Preservation Act of 1996, as amended:** Instructs federal agencies to consider the effect their undertakings have on cultural resources. Section 106, outlines a procedure to accommodate historic preservation concerns with the needs of Federal undertakings through a process of information gathering and consultation.

**National Wildlife Refuge System Improvement Act of 1997:** Sets the mission and administrative policy for all refuges in the National Wildlife Refuge System; mandates comprehensive conservation planning for all units of the National Wildlife Refuge System.

**Endangered Species Act (1973):** Requires all Federal agencies to carry out programs for the conservation of endangered and threatened species.

**National Environmental Policy Act (1969):** Requires all agencies, including the Service, to examine the environmental impacts of their actions, incorporate environmental information, and use public participation in the planning and implementation of all actions. Federal agencies must integrate this Act with other planning requirements, and prepare appropriate documents to facilitate better environmental decision making (from 40 CFR 1500).

**National Wildlife Refuge System Administration Act (1966):** Defines the National Wildlife Refuge System and authorizes the Secretary to permit any use of a refuge, provided such use is compatible with the major purposes for which the refuge was established.

**Refuge Recreation Act (1962):** Allows the use of refuges for recreation when such uses are compatible with the refuge's primary purposes and when sufficient funds are available to manage the uses.

**Fish and Wildlife Coordination Act (1958):** Allows the Fish and Wildlife Service to enter into agreements with private landowners for wildlife management purposes.

**Migratory Bird Conservation Act (1929):** Establishes procedures for acquisition by purchase, rental, or gifts of areas approved by the Migratory Bird Conservation Commission.

**Migratory Bird Treaty Act (1918):** Designates the protection of migratory birds as a Federal responsibility. This Act enables the setting of seasons and other regulations, including the closing of areas, Federal or non-Federal, to the hunting of migratory birds.

## PUBLIC SCOPING

Public scoping was completed in December 2004. A public meeting was held in Sturgis, South Dakota, on December 2, 2004. Two people attended this meeting and in addition five written comments were received during the open-comment period. Comments received identified biological, social, and economic concerns regarding management. These comments were considered during preparation of the draft comprehensive conservation plan/environmental assessment (CCP/EA).

## PUBLIC COMMENTS

A draft CCP/EA was developed and released for public review and comment in February 2007. An open house was held in Sturgis on February 28, 2007, at the Community Center. Ten individuals attended representing state, county, tribal, local conservation, and landowner interests. In addition, nearly 90 comment letters were received as well as phone calls. All comments were reviewed and taken into consideration by the planning team.

Eight-six review and comment letters were received. Ten were received from government agencies and/or officials, tribal governments, and conservation organizations. The remaining 76 letters were received from the public, with a large number being from individual tribal members.

## RESPONSE TO PUBLIC COMMENTS

**Comment 1:** Pages 8, 9, 10, and 24 misidentify landscape components. They are cultural resources.

**Response:** Agree. The text has been clarified.

**Comment 2:** Please state that Bear Butte was designated a National Historic Landmark in 1981.

**Response:** Agree. The information has been added.

**Comment 3:** Concern was expressed regarding turning over management responsibility to the state of South Dakota, Bureau of Land Management, and private landowners.

**Response:** These agencies have provided for management of the site according to their mandates, in particular, the 1967 cooperative agreement with the state.

**Comment 4:** The EA did not discuss a full range of alternatives and should propose another alternative expanding the USFWS presence.

**Response:** A full range of alternatives were considered, including transferring the easements to another entity and expanding the role of the USFWS at Bear Butte

NWR. These two options were not further developed after determining they either were not allowed or were not feasible.

**Comment 5:** The draft EA provides insufficient documentation of the existence of conflicts between recreation and wildlife.

**Response:** There is very limited data available on wildlife use at the site.

**Comment 6:** Despite the USFWS mission for the conservation of wildlife, non-wildlife-dependent public uses are being allowed.

**Response:** A use is not automatically restricted if it is not one of the priority public uses of hunting, fishing, wildlife observation, photography, environmental education, and interpretation. Non-wildlife-dependent recreation, such as camping and swimming, have been allowed since establishment and are part of the establishing purposes as evidenced in several of the easements. Again, the area is managed according to the 1967 cooperative agreement.

**Comment 7:** Removal of USFWS interests will seriously threaten the protection of Native American interests. Divestiture will result in further encroachment of development that will harm Mato Paha (Bear Butte), considered a sacred place. Culturally inappropriate development is not mentioned in the "Environmental Justice" section of the EA.

**Response:** The USFWS has no authority outside the limited-interest easements it holds.

**Comment 8:** Tribal consultation did not occur, nor was it sought.

**Response:** Tribal consultation did occur at the Lacreek open house held in Martin, South Dakota, in 2004, attended by members of the Rosebud and Oglala Sioux tribes and the South Dakota Game, Fish, and Parks Department (SDGFP), and at the open house attended by members of several tribes and Bear Butte State Park staff in April 2004 (mentioned in draft CCP). All tribes were invited to the refuge open house in Sturgis in March 2004, but no one attended. The refuge wildlife biologist also met with all game and fish department representatives from the Dakotas, Montana, and Nebraska at the Native American Fish and Wildlife Society Great Plains conference in Rapid City, South Dakota, in March 2004. In addition, the regional director of the USFWS region 6 sent formal invitations to participate in the planning process to the tribal chairmen and tribal committees from 24 Plains tribes listed in appendix C.

**Comment 9:** An environmental impact statement (EIS) should be prepared, as the affected areas have "unique characteristics."

*Response:* The USFWS does not believe development of an EIS is warranted in this case.

**Comment 10:** There is a hope that the USFWS will acquire more land and conservation easements in the area.

*Response:* The USFWS has no interest in acquiring more land or easements in the area.

**Comment 11:** Please improve the map of the refuge to more clearly depict ownership.

*Response:* The map will be edited for the final CCP.

**Comment 12:** Discuss the effects of your plans on the heron rookery.

*Response:* It was reported that a heron rookery exists in the area. Our final CCP has adopted the current management scenario. No change in management is proposed.

**Comment 13:** Please provide more detail on the cooperative agreement with the state.

*Response:* A long history of cooperation exists between the USFWS and the state of South Dakota in management of Bear Butte NWR. The state acquired the majority of lands from private landowners and established Bear Butte State Park. Shortly thereafter, a more formal cooperative agreement was established, which provided for the state to manage the limited-interest easements in consultation with the USFWS (refer to appendix F).

**Comment 14:** The CCP fails to discuss cumulative impacts.

*Response:* Based on the limited management responsibilities at Bear Butte NWR, environmental impacts are extremely limited. Particularly in light of the fact that the USFWS has designated alternative A—current management (no action) as the preferred alternative (final CCP).

**Comment 15:** The CCP does not include a Section 7 evaluation.

*Response:* A Section 7 consultation is a formal review between the refuge staff and the ecological services office of the USFWS to determine if any proposed actions may affect species that have been formally listed as federally threatened or endangered. A Section 7 consultation, which was completed for the draft CCP/EA, determined that no effects to threatened or endangered species known to use the site will result. The final signed Section 7 is generally included with the final CCP. Since the final CCP has adopted a current management scenario, and no changes are proposed, a revised Section 7 consultation is not warranted.

**Comment 16:** Concern was expressed regarding a proposed highway bypass and its impact on potential commercial development on lands near Bear Butte.

*Response:* During the planning phase for this proposed highway bypass, a similar public review process will likely be required, as federal dollars will likely fund a significant share of the project.

## MAILING LIST

The following mailing list was developed for this CCP:

### FEDERAL OFFICIALS

U.S. Representative Stephanie Herseth, Washington DC, Rapid City, SD, Area Director

U.S. Senator Tim Johnson, Washington DC, Rapid City, SD, Area Director

U.S. Senator John Thune, Washington DC, Rapid City, SD, Area Director

### FEDERAL AGENCIES LOCATED IN SOUTH DAKOTA

Bureau of Land Management, South Dakota Field Office, Belle Fourche

U.S. Fish and Wildlife Service Ecological Services, Pierre

National Park Service, Omaha, NE

National Park Service, Interior

USDA Forest Service, Black Hills National Forest, Custer

USDA Forest Service, Chadron, NE

### TRIBAL ORGANIZATIONS

Arapaho Business Council, Fort Washakie, WY

Black Feet Tribal Business Council, Browning, MT

Cheyenne River Sioux Tribe, Eagle Butte, SD

Chippewa Cree Business Committee, Box Elder, MT

Crow Creek Sioux Tribal Council, Fort Thompson, SD

Crow Tribal Council, Crow Agency, MT

Flandreau Santee Sioux Executive Committee, Flandreau, SD

Fort Belknap Community Council, Harlem, MT

Fort Peck Tribal Executive Board, Popular, MT

Lower Bruele Sioux Tribal Council, Lower Brule, SD

Northern Cheyenne Tribal Council, Lame Deer, MT 59043

Oglala Sioux Tribal Council, Pine Ridge, SD

Omaha Tribal Council, Macy, NE

Ponca Tribe of Nebraska, Niobrara, NE

Rosebud Sioux Tribal Council, Rosebud, SD

Santee Sioux Tribal Council, Niobrara, NE

Shoshone Business Council, Fort Washakie, WY

Sisseton-Wahpeton Sioux Tribe, Agency Village, SD

Spirit Lake Tribal Council, Fort Totten, ND

Standing Rock Sioux Tribe, Fort Yates, ND

Three Affiliated Tribes, New Town, ND

Tribal Preservation Office, Standing Rock Sioux Tribe, Fort Yates, ND

Winnebago Tribal Council, Winnebago, NE

Yankton Sioux Tribe, Marty, SD

## SOUTH DAKOTA STATE OFFICIALS

Office of the Governor, Pierre

Senator Cooper Garnos, Preesho

Senator Theresa Two Bull, Pine Ridge

Senator Kenneth McNenny, Sturgis

Senator J.P. Duniphan, Rapid City

Representative Jim Bradford, Pine Ridge

Representative Betty Olson, Prairie City

Representative Thomas Brunner, Nisland

Representative Larry Rhoden, Union Center

Representative Michael Buckingham, Rapid City

Representative Don Van Etten, Rapid City

## SOUTH DAKOTA STATE AGENCIES

Department of Agriculture, Pierre

Department of Emergency Management, Pierre

Department of Environment and Natural Resources, Pierre

Department of Game, Fish and Parks, Pierre, Sturgis, Rosebud and Lead

Division of Water Rights, Pierre

State Historic Preservation Officer, Pierre

State Conservationist, Pierre

Farm Bureau Federation, Huron

## SOUTH DAKOTA LOCAL AGENCIES

City of Sturgis, South Dakota

Meade County Conservation District, Sturgis

Meade County Government, Sturgis

## INTEREST GROUPS

Izaak Walton League, Washington DC

The Humane Society of the U.S., Washington DC

Sierra Club-Black Hills Group, Rapid City

Audubon Society-Prairie Hills Chapter, Black Hawk

Animal Welfare Institute, Washington DC

Porcupine School, Porcupine

## INDIVIDUALS

(68 people)

## Environmental Action Statement
U.S. Fish and Wildlife Service, Region 6
Lakewood, Colorado

Within the spirit and intent of the Council on Environmental Quality's regulations for implementing the National Environmental Policy Act and other statutes, orders, and policies that protect fish and wildlife resources, I have established the following administrative record.I have determined that the action of implementing the Comprehensive Conservation Plan for Bear Butte National Wildlife Refuge is found not to have significant environmental effects, as determined by the attached finding of no significant impact and the environmental assessment.

Stephen Guertin                          Date
Regional Director, Region 6
U.S. Fish and Wildlife Service
Lakewood, CO

Richard A. Coleman, PhD                  Date
Assistant Regional Director, Region 6
National Wildlife Refuge System
U.S. Fish and Wildlife Service
Lakewood, CO

Rod Krey                                 Date
Refuge Supervisor (KS, ND, NE, SD)
U.S. Fish and Wildlife Service, Region 6
Lakewood, CO

Tom Koerner                              Date
Refuge Manager
Bear Butte National Wildlife Refuge
Martin, SD

# Finding of No Significant Impact
U.S. Fish and Wildlife Service, Region 6
Lakewood, Colorado

Two management alternatives for Bear Butte National Wildlife Refuge (NWR) comprehensive conservation plan (CCP) were assessed as to their effectiveness in achieving the refuge's purposes and their impact on the human environment. Alternative A—current management (no action), which is now the preferred alternative, will continue current management of the refuge. Under this alternative, existing habitat within the limited-interest easement and all public use programs will continue to be administered and maintained by the South Dakota Game, Fish, and Parks Department per the 1967 cooperative agreement. Alternative B proposed that easements will be relinquished to current landowners and that the U.S. Fish and Wildlife Service will divest its interests. Bear Butte NWR will be taken out of the National Wildlife Refuge System and the easements will be transferred to the current landowners.

The preferred alternative (alternative A) was selected because it best meets the purposes for which Bear Butte NWR was established and is preferable to alternative B in light of physical, biological, economic, and social factors. During preparation and review of the draft comprehensive conservation plan and environmental assessment, alternative B was the proposed action, in keeping with a long history of proposing divestiture of this limited-interest refuge. However, after reviewing public comments, evaluating new information, and further analysis, the final CCP adopted alternative A—no action.

I find that the preferred alternative is not a major federal action that will significantly affect the quality of the human environment within the meaning of Section 102(2) (C) of the National Environmental Policy Act of 1969. Accordingly, the preparation of an environmental impact statement on the proposed action is not required.

The following is a summary of anticipated environmental effects from implementation of the preferred alternative. The preferred alternative will not:

- adversely impact endangered or threatened species or their habitat

- adversely impact archaeological or historical resources

- adversely impact wetlands nor does the plan call for structures that could be damaged by or that will significantly influence the movement of floodwater

- have a disproportionately high or adverse human health or environmental effect on minority or low-income populations

The state of South Dakota has been notified and given the opportunity to review the CCP and associated environmental assessment.

_____          9/24/07
Stephen Guertin                             Date
Regional Director, Region 6
U.S. Fish and Wildlife Service
Lakewood, CO

## BIRDS

### Loons and Grebes

Common loon
Western grebe
Horned grebe
Eared grebe
Pied-billed grebe

### Pelicans and Cormorants

American white pelican
Double-crested cormorant

### Geese and Ducks

Canada goose
Greater white-fronted goose
Snow goose
Mallard
Northern pintail
Gadwall
American wigeon
Northern shoveler
Blue-winged teal
Cinnamon teal
Green-winged teal
Wood duck
Redhead
Canvasback
Ring-necked duck
Lesser scaup
Common goldeneye
Bufflehead
Old squaw
White-winged scoter
Hooded merganser
Red-breasted merganser
Common merganser
Ruddy duck

### Vultures, Hawks, and Eagles

Turkey vulture
Cooper's hawk
Sharp-shinned hawk
Northern harrier

Rough-legged hawk
Ferruginous hawk
Red-tailed hawk
Swainson's hawk
Broad-winged hawk
Bald eagle
Golden eagle
Osprey
Prairie falcon
American kestrel
Merlin

### Gallinaceous Birds

Wild turkey
Sharp-tailed grouse
Ring-necked pheasant
Gray partridge

### Herons

Great blue heron
Green-backed heron
Yellow-crowned night-heron

### Cranes, Rails, and Coots

Sandhill crane
Sora rail
American coot

### Shorebirds

American avocet
Black-bellied plover
Piping plover
Killdeer
Marbled godwit
Long-billed curlew
Greater yellowlegs
Lesser yellowlegs
Solitary sandpiper
Upland sandpiper
Willet
Spotted sandpiper
Short-billed dowitcher
Lon-billed dowitcher
Wilson's phalarope

Common snipe
Least sandpiper
Semi-palmated sandpiper
Western sandpiper

### Gulls and Terns

Ring-billed gull
Franklin gull
Common tern
Forster's tern
Black tern

### Pigeons and Doves

Rock dove
Mourning dove

### Cuckoos

Yellow-billed cuckoo
Black-billed cuckoo

### Owls

Screech owl
Great horned owl
Lon-eared owl
Short-eared owl
Snow owl
Northern saw-whet

### Goatsuckers, Swifts, and Kingfishers

Common nighthawk
Chimney swift
Belted kingfisher

### Woodpeckers

Lewis' woodpecker
Red-headed woodpecker
Downy woodpecker
Hairy woodpecker
Northern flicker

### Flycatchers

Eastern kingbird
Western kingbird
Say's phoebe
Least flycatcher
Western flycatcher

Trail's flycatcher
Western wood pewee
Olive-sided flycatcher

### Larks

Horned lark

### Swallows

Barn swallow
Cliff swallow
Violet-green swallow
Tree swallow
Bank swallow
Northern rough-winged swallow

### Corvids

Blue jay
Gray jay
Black-billed magpie
American crow

### Chickadees, Nuthatches, and Creepers

Black-capped chickadee
White-breasted nuthatch
Red-breasted nuthatch
Brown creeper

### Wrens

House wren
Rock wren
Canyon wren
Marsh wren

### Thrashers and Thrushes

Gray catbird
Brown thrasher
American robin
Townsend's solitaire
Veery
Eastern bluebird
Mountain bluebird

### Kinglets, Pipits, and Waxwings

Ruby-crowned kinglet

Water pipit
Bohemian waxwing
Cedar waxwing

## Shrikes and Starlings

Northern shrike
Loggerhead shrike
European starling

## Vireos and Warblers

Solitary vireo
Red-eyed vireo
Warbling vireo
Black-and-white warbler
Orange-crowned warbler
Yellow warbler
Yellow-rumped warbler
   Myrtle race
   Audubon race
Ovenbird
Common yellow-throat
Yellow-breasted chat
American redstart
Chestnut-sided warbler
Blue-gray gnatcatcher
Blue-winged warbler

## Weaver Finches

House sparrow

## Blackbirds and Orioles

Bobolink
Western meadowlark
Yellow-headed blackbird
Red-winged blackbird
Brewer's blackbird
Common grackle
Brown-headed cowbird
Orchard oriole
Northern oriole

## Tanagers, Grosbeaks, and Others

Western tanager

Rose-breasted grosbeak
Black-headed grosbeak
Evening grosbeak
Blue grosbeak
Indigo bunting
Lazuli bunting
Rosy finch
Common redpoll
Pine siskin
American goldfinch
Red crossbill
Rufous-sided towhee

## Sparrows and Longspurs

Savannah sparrow
Grasshopper sparrow
Lark bunting
Vesper sparrow
Lark sparrow
Dark-eyed junco
   Slate-colored race
   White-winged race
   Oregon race
American tree sparrow
Chipping sparrow
Clay-colored sparrow
Field sparrow
Harris's sparrow
White-crowned sparrow
White-throated sparrow
Song sparrow
Chestnut-collared longspur

COOPERATIVE AGREEMENT

THIS AGREEMENT entered into between the Department of the
Interior through the Fish and Wildlife Service, hereinafter referred to
as the Service, and the State of South Dakota, Department of Game, Fish,
and Parks, hereinafter referred to as the State, witnesseth that:

WHEREAS the Service, pursuant to the Act of Congress approved
August 14, 1946 (60 Stat. 1080; 16 U.S.C. 661-666c), is authorized to
provide assistance to and cooperate with State agencies in the development,
protection, rearing, and stocking of all species of wildlife, resources
thereof, and their habitat; and

WHEREAS, the Service, pursuant to the terms and conditions of,
and under the rights granted in eight (8) Easements and one (1) License
to the United States, from the State and private parties, now operates
and maintains an area for migratory bird, wildlife conservation and other
purposes, known as the Bear Butte Lake Project in Meade County, South Dakota;
and

WHEREAS it is the desire of the parties to this agreement to
cooperate in the continued operation and maintenance of said project; and

WHEREAS the State represents itself as authorized and willing
to assume the responsibility and cost of maintaining and operating the
aforesaid Bear Butte Lake Project;

NOW THEREFORE, it is mutually agreed, in consideration of the
covenants and releases hereinafter contained, that

1. The State will administer, operate and maintain the Bear Butte
Lake Project pursuant to the rights and interest in real property heretofore
acquired by the United States in connection with the said Bear Butte Lake

Project, Meade County, South Dakota, and more particularly described and set forth in the eight (8) Easements and one (1) License identified as Tracts (2P), (4 ), (5P), (7F), (8F), (8M), (9F), and (11P), copies of which are attached hereto and made a part hereof.

2. The State agrees to report annually not later than August 1 to the Director of the Fish and Wildlife Service as to the use or non-use of the above-described lands for the purposes herein specified during the preceding fiscal year ending June 30.

3. The State agrees to notify promptly the Service, through the Regional Director, of any intention to relinquish administration of the project.

4. No member of or delegate to Congress or resident commissioner shall be admitted to any share or part of this agreement, or to any benefit to arise therefrom, separate and apart from any benefit accruing to the general public.

5. This agreement shall become effective as of the date of a letter of notice from the Service informing the State that execution of the agreement has been completed and that the above-described lands are available for administration by the State.

IN WITNESS WHEREOF, the parties have executed this cooperative agreement on the day, month, and year opposite their signatures thereto.

_July 12_, 1967

The State of South Dakota

by _R J Hodgins_
Director, Department of Game, Fish and Parks

_Aug. 1_, 1967

The United States of America
Department of the Interior

by _____
Director, Fish and Wildlife Service

**Name:** Bear Butte National Wildlife Easement Refuge

## Establishing and Acquisition Authority:

- Migratory Bird Conservation Act 45 Stat 1222;

- Executive Order, August 26, 1935, *"as a refuge and breeding ground for migratory birds and other wildlife."*

- Migratory Bird Conservation Act *"for use as an inviolate sanctuary, or for any other management purpose, for migratory birds."*

## Refuge Purposes:

"For use as an inviolate sanctuary, or for any other management purpose, for migratory birds." USC 715d (Migratory Bird Conservation Act)

## National Wildlife Refuge System Mission:

*The mission of the System is to administer a national network of lands and waters for the conservation, management, and where appropriate, restoration of the fish, wildlife, and plant resources and their habitats within the United States for the benefit of present and future generations of Americans.*

**Mandatory 15-year Reevaluation Date:** 2022

## 1. Description of Proposed Use: Environmental Education and Interpretation

**Provide Opportunities for Environmental Education and Interpretation:** Environmental education consists of activities conducted by South Dakota Game, Fish, and Parks staff, refuge staff, volunteers, and teachers. Interpretation occurs in less formal activities with refuge staff volunteers or through exhibits, educational trunks, signs, and brochures. Currently, environmental education and interpretation activities are entirely conducted by staff and volunteers from Bear Butte State Park, who provide tours and interpretation for a variety of groups.

**Availability of Resources:** Continuance of environmental education and interpretation will remain entirely up to the discretion of the SDGFP and its volunteers.

**Anticipated Impacts of Use:** Minimal disturbances to wildlife and wildlife habitat will result from these uses at the current and proposed levels. Adverse impacts are minimized through careful timing and placement of activities. Some disturbance to wildlife will occur in areas frequented by visitors. There will be some minor damage to vegetation, littering, and increased maintenance. Location and time limitations placed on environmental education and interpretation activities will ensure that this activity will have only minor impacts on wildlife and will not detract from the primary purposes of the refuge.

No cultural resources will be impacted negatively, only positively through education. No impact to endangered species should occur.

**Determination:** Environmental education and interpretation are compatible.

**Stipulations Necessary to Ensure Compatibility:**

- Allow environmental education and interpretation under the guidance of SDGFP staff, a volunteer or a trained teacher to ensure minimal disturbance to wildlife, minimal damage to vegetation, and minimal conflicts between groups

**Justification:** Based on biological impacts described in the environmental assessment (EA) and the final CCP, it is determined that environmental education and interpretation within the Bear Butte National Wildlife Refuge will not materially interfere with or detract from the purposes for which this refuge was established.

Environmental education and interpretation are priority public uses listed in the National Wildlife Refuge System Improvement Act of 1997. By facilitating environmental education, refuge visitors will gain knowledge and an appreciation of fish, wildlife, and their habitats, whish will lead to increased public awareness and stewardship of natural resources. Increased appreciation for natural resources will support and complement the Service's actions in achieving the purposes of the refuge and the mission of the Refuge System.

**Mandatory 15-year Reevaluation Date:** 2022

## 2. Description of Proposed Use: Wildlife Observation and Wildlife Photography

Provide Opportunities that Support Wildlife-dependent Recreation: Wildlife observation and wildlife photography are facilitated by two hiking trails.

The CCP proposes to continue the above uses, which are entirely provided for and maintained by the SDGFP.

**Availability of Resources:** The availability of this use will be entirely at the discretion of the SDGFP.

Determination: Wildlife observation and wildlife photography are compatible.

**Stipulations Necessary to Ensure Compatibility:**

- Monitor use, regulate access, and maintain necessary facilities to prevent habitat degradation and minimize wildlife disturbance

**Justification:** Based on the anticipated biological impacts above and in the EA, it is determined that wildlife observation and wildlife photography on the Bear Butte National Wildlife Refuge will not interfere with the habitat goals and objectives or purposes for which it was established.

Wildlife observation and wildlife photography are priority public uses listed in the Improvement Act. By facilitating these uses, visitors will gain knowledge and an appreciation of fish and wildlife, which will lead to increased public stewardship of wildlife and their habitats. Increased public stewardship will support and complement the Service's actions in achieving the purposes of the refuge and the mission of the Refuge System.

**Mandatory 15-year Reevaluation Date:** 2022

### 3. Description of Use: Recreational Fishing

Continue to Provide for Recreational Fishing at Designated Fishing Areas in Accordance with State Regulations.

Currently, the fisheries resource is non existent, due to ongoing drought. It is possible, that future runoff events may fill the lake to levels where a fisheries resource may be restocked. The stocking and subsequent management of the fishery will be entirely at the discretion of the SDGFP.

**Availability of Resources:** If a fisheries is reestablished, it will be entirely administered by SDGFP staff. The CCP does not call for the implementation of any new fishing programs.

**Anticipated Impacts of Use:** Fishing and other human activities may cause some disturbance to migratory birds and other wildlife. Disturbance caused by fishing pressure will vary with availability of the resource and the ability to use boats. Currently, no fishing or boating activity is possible due to ongoing drought and low lake levels, which will eliminate disturbance issues for waterbirds. A large share of migratory bird species prefer shallow water levels, and their use will be expected to rise with the shallow lake levels. Once water returns, and deeper lake levels permit re-establishment of a fisheries, bird use for most species will decline. Disturbance potential will be reduced, due to reduced habitat suitability for most migratory bird species.

**Determination:** Recreational fishing is compatible.

Stipulations Necessary to Ensure Compatibility:

- Require that fishing follow state and federal regulations

**Justification:** Based on the biological impacts addressed above and in the EA, it is determined recreational fishing will not materially interfere with the habitat goals and objectives or purposes for refuge establishment.

Fishing is a priority public use as listed in the National Wildlife Refuge System Improvement Act of 1997.

**Mandatory 15-year Reevaluation Date:** 2022

### 4. Description of Use: Recreational Hunting

Allow recreational hunting for all legal species according to state regulations.

**Availability of Resources:** Currently, the SDGFP administers the recreational hunting program.

**Anticipated Impacts of Use:** Some wildlife disturbance will occur during recreational hunting activities at the refuge. Other public use activities such as boating, swimming, and recreational fishing will be minimally impacted by recreational hunting.

Determination: Recreational hunting is compatible.

Stipulations Necessary to Ensure Compatibility:

- Require the use of nontoxic shot, in accordance with current regulations for migratory bird hunting
- Continue to prohibit hunting within the developed campground sites.
- Require that hunting be in accordance with federal and state regulations

**Justification:** Hunting on national wildlife refuges has been identified as a priority public use in the National Wildlife Refuge System Improvement Act of 1997. Hunting is a legitimate wildlife management tool that can be used to manage populations. Hunting harvests a small percentage of the renewable resources, which is in accordance with wildlife objectives and principles.

Based on the biological impacts anticipated above and in the EA, it is determined that recreational hunting at Bear Butte easement National Wildlife Refuge will not materially interfere with or detract from the purposes for which this refuge was established or its habitat goals and objectives.

**Mandatory 15-year Reevaluation Date:** 2022

### 5. Description of Proposed Public Use: Boating, Swimming, Picknicking, and Camping

Continue recreational activities including boating, swimming, picknicking, and camping in accordance with state and refuge regulations.

Boating, swimming, picnicking, and camping have been allowed at Bear Butte easement NWR since it was created. Easements taken also include recreational developments, indicating these were included in the purposes for establishment.

**Availability of Resources:** These activities are provided for and maintained entirely by the SDGFP, as they are the land owners and manage the site as part of Bear Butte State Park. Facilities and programs are adequately maintained. Continuance of these programs is entirely at the discretion of the SDGFP.

**Anticipated Impacts of the Use**: Recreational activities proposed will likely provide some disturbance to wildlife and wildlife habitat. Increased public use activities may create disturbance to nesting waterfowl and other wildlife.

**Determination**: Boating, swimming, picnicking, and camping at Bear Butte easement NWR are compatible.

**Stipulations Necessary to Ensure Compatibility:**

■ Activities are conducted in accordance with state and refuge regulations

**Justification**: These activities have been allowed since establishment and are part of the purposes for establishment.

**Mandatory 15-year Reevaluation Date: 2022**

## Signature

Tom Koerner, Refuge Manager          08/13/2007
Bear Butte easement NWR                      Date
Martin, SD

## Review

Lloyd Jones                                          8/16/07
Regional Compatibility Coordinator      Date
USFWS, Region 6

Rod Krey                                             8/20/07
Refuge Program Supervisor                   Date
(ND, SD, NE, KS)
USFWS, Region 6

## Concurrence

Richard A. Coleman, PhD          8/29/07
Assistant Regional Director         Date
National Wildlife Refuge System
USFWS, Region 6

# Bibliography

# Bibliography

Bureau of Land Management and South Dakota Game, Fish, and Parks Department. 1991. Birds of the Fort Meade Recreation Area and Bear Butte State Park. Bear Butte State Park, SD.

"Black Hills" encyclopedia entry in Wikipedia. <http://www.en.wikipedia.org/wiki/Black_Hills> accessed 1/15/05

Green, J.; and Short, N.M. 1971. Volcanic landforms and surface features: a photographic atlas and glossary. NY: Springer Verlag. 519 p.

Karner, F.R.; and Halvorson, D.L. 1987. The Devils Tower, Bear Lodge Mountains: cenozoic igneous complex. In Beus, S.S., ed., Centennial field guide. Volume 2. Geological Society of America, Rocky Mountain Section. 161–164.

National Park Service entry for Wind Cave National Park. <http://www.nps.gov/wica/Grasses_of_the_Mixed_Grass_Prairie.htm> 2/15/06

South Dakota Game, Fish, and Parks Department. 2003. South Dakota Statewide Fisheries Survey 2102-F21-R-36. Pierre, SD.

"Sturgis, South Dakota" encyclopedia entry in Wikipedia. <http://en.wikipedia.org/wiki/Sturgis%2C_South_Dakota>

U.S. Census Bureau Quick Facts. 2002.

U.S. Fish and Wildlife Service (USFWS). 2002. Birds of conservation concern. U.S. Fish and Wildlife Service, Division of Migratory Bird Management. Arlington, VA. <http://migratorybirds.fws.gov/reports/BCC2002.pdf>

————. 2005. Draft comprehensive conservation plan and environmental assessment, Kirwin National Wildlife Refuge. Denver, CO.

USFWS, Chief, Division of Realty, Region 6. Memo dated May 26, 2004. U.S. Fish and Wildlife Service.